H-1B Specialty Occupation Visa

ATTORNEY BRIAN D. LERNER

Law Offices of Brian D. Lerner, A Professional Corporation

Attorney Brian D. Lerner

H-1B Specialty Occupation Visa

H-1B Specialty Occupation Visa

Written by Attorney Brian D. Lerner

Print ISBN: 978-1-948774-86-4
Ebook ISBN: 978-1-948774-85-7

INTRODUCTION

There are a multitude of different immigration petitions and applications. They are complex and full of requirements. Obviously it would be best to hire and immigration attorney to best prepare the petitions and application. However, this can certainly cost thousands of dollars.

The next best option is to get a sample of the petition written by an experienced immigration attorney. The samples cost a fraction what would be charged by an immigration attorney. However, while the reader has to alter, amend and change the parts of the sample petition to reflect their actual situation, it is a fantastic roadmap for them to use. If the reader has purchased the entire petition or application, they will have real live samples of cover letters, forms, declarations, affidavits and the necessary exhibits to use. The samples come from real cases and the names of those clients have been redacted to protect the privacy of that person or corporation.

These are petitions and applications that have been drafted by an experienced immigration attorney with over 25 years of experience. Get the benefits of that experience without the costs.

About the Law Offices of Brian D. Lerner

Brian D. Lerner has been a licensed attorney since 1992 and started the Law Offices of Brian D. Lerner, APC. The law practice consists of Immigration and Nationality Law and everything involved with and regarding immigration which includes citizenship, investment visas, family and employment visas, removal and deportation hearings, appeals, waivers, adjustment, consulate processing and all types of immigration and citizenship matters. Thousands of families have been reunited and/or permitted to stay in the U.S. and/or return to the U.S. because of the successful work of Immigration Attorney Brian D. Lerner.

This law offices handles all types of immigration cases including family based and employment based. Immigration issues range from immigration court proceedings to trying to fix what paralegals may have done that was neither correct nor proper. Foreign nationals must have experience lawyers admitted to practice law.

The Law Offices of Brian D. Lerner, APC, handles cases arising from business visas, work permits, Green Cards, non-immigrant visas, deportation, citizenship, appeals and all areas of immigration. The Law Offices of Brian D. Lerner, APC does EB-5 Investor Visas, H-1B Specialty Occupation, L-1 Intracompany Transferee, E-2 Treaty Investor, E-1 Treaty Trader, O-1 Extraordinary Ability among others. Regarding immigrant visas for the Green Card, the firm does PERM and advanced degree PERM, Family Petitions, and Extraordinary Alien Petitions. In addition to affirmative petitions, the Law Firm represents people in deportation and removal hearings, including political asylum, withholding of removal, and convention against torture cases.

Brian D. Lerner has been certified as an expert in Immigration & Nationality Law by the California State Bar, Board of Legal Specialization sicne 2000 and has been re-certified three times. He now passes on his decades of experience by allowing the Reader, Law Schools, Professors and other Immigration Attorneys to purchase sample petitions on every facet of Immigration Law.

TABLE OF CONTENTS

ABOUT THE H-1B

Do you have a college degree? The H-1B is the best type of work visa for you to obtain. However, they are used up very quickly each year. If your not going to have an attorney help you, you should use this book to get a clear and concise example of what is needed. There are many parts to a successful H-1B and this book makes it much easier to put it all together for submission before the deadline.

SECTION 1
Attorney Cover Letter

LAW OFFICES OF
BRIAN D. LERNER
A PROFESSIONAL CORPORATION

BRIAN D. LERNER, ESQ.
CERTIFIED SPECIALIST IN IMMIGRATION AND NATIONALITY LAW

WWW.CALIFORNIAIMMIGRATION.US

ADMITTED TO THE UNITED STATES SUPREME COURT
ADMITTED TO THE U.S. COURTS OF APPEALS FOR THE 1ST THROUGH 11TH CIRCUITS

3233 EAST BROADWAY . LONG BEACH, CALIFORNIA 90803 . TELEPHONE (562) 495-0554 . FACSIMILE (562) 608-8672

March 31, 2015

California Service Center
U.S. Citizenship and Immigration Services
Attn: I-129 (H-1B)
24000 Avila Road, 2nd Floor, Room 2312
Laguna Niguel, CA 92677

Re: Form: I-129, Petition for a Nonimmigrant Worker (H-1B)
Petitioner: Inland Empire Liver Foundation
Beneficiary:

Dear Officer:

We enclose the following forms and fees with this petition:

- Form G-28, Notice of Entry of Appearance as Attorney or Accredited Representative (Petitioner);
- Form G-28, Notice of Entry of Appearance as Attorney or Accredited Representative (Beneficiary);
- Form I-129, Petition for a Nonimmigrant Worker;
- Form I-129 Supplement H;
- Form I-129 H-1B Data Collection and Filing Fee Exemption Supplement; and
- Filing Fees in the Amount of \$325, \$500 and \$750.

We submit copies of the following exhibits with this petition:

Table of Exhibits

Exhibits	**Description**
1.	Beneficiary's Passport and I-94;
2.	Beneficiary's Bachelor of Pharmacy & Pharmaceutical Chemistry Degree and General Evaluation Report;
3.	Beneficiary's Resume;
4.	Letter from Petitioner;
5.	Petitioner's Business Tax Certificate;

6. Petitioner's ByLaws;
7. Labor Condition Application;
8. Online Wage Library;
9. Occupational Outlook Handbook;
10. O*Net OnLine Summary; and
11. Sample Job Advertisements.

Petitioner, Inland Empire Liver Foundation, through undersigned counsel, respectfully requests H-1B nonimmigrant status for Beneficiary, ████████ ████████ Specifically, Petitioner seeks to employ Beneficiary for a three-year period in a specialty occupation as a Research Chemist.

I.
H-1B NONIMMIGRANT STATUS

H-1B status applies to an alien who is coming temporarily to the United States to perform services in a specialty occupation, that meets the requirements of section 214(i)(2) of the Immigration and Nationality Act (hereinafter "INA" or "Act") and for whom the Department of Labor has determined and certified to the Attorney General that the prospective employer has filed a labor condition application.[1]

H-1B status may be granted to an alien who will perform services in a specialty occupation which requires theoretical and practical application of a body of highly specialized knowledge and attainment of a bachelor's or higher degree or its equivalent as a minimum requirement for entry into the occupation in the United States and who is qualified to perform services on the specialty occupation because he or she has attained a Bachelor or higher degree or its equivalent in the specialty occupation.[2]

The maximum period of validity for an initial H-1B is three years.[3] Extensions of stay up to three additional years are available.[4] Generally, the total period stay may not exceed six years.[5]

In the present case, Beneficiary is currently in F-1 status and has never been granted H-1B status. Therefore, Beneficiary is eligible for a three-year H-1B. **Exhibits 1.**

II.
THE POSITION OF RESEARCH CHEMIST IS A SPECIALTY OCCUPATION.

To qualify as a specialty occupation, the position must meet one of the following criteria:

(1) A bachelor's or higher degree or its equivalent is normally the minimum requirement for entry into the particular position;
(2) The degree requirement is common in the industry in parallel positions among similar organizations;
(3) The employer normally requires a degree or its equivalent for the position; or
(4) The nature of the duties is so specialized and complex that the

[1] 8 C.F.R. § 214.2(h)(i)(B)(1).
[2] 8 C.F.R. § 214.2(h)(4)(i)(A)(1).
[3] 8 C.F.R. § 214.2(h)(9)(iii).
[4] 8 C.F.R. § 214.2(h)(15)(ii)(B)(1).
[5] Id.

> knowledge required to perform the duties is usually associated with the attainment of a bachelor's or higher degree.[6]

In the present case, a bachelor's degree or its equivalent is normally the minimum requirement for entry in the particular position. **Exhibits 4, 8-11.** The Occupational Information Network ("O*NET") classifies this position under Zone 4, category 19-2031.00. **Exhibit 10.** Regarding Zone Four, O*NET states, "[m]ost of these occupations require a four-year bachelor's degree." **Exhibit 10.**

Further, a bachelor's degree or its equivalent in this specific field is commonly required in parallel positions in similar organizations. **Exhibits 4, 8-11.**

Also, Petitioner normally requires a four-year degree or its equivalent for this kind of work. **Exhibit 4.**

Finally, the nature of the beneficiary's duties will be so specialized or complex that the knowledge to perform them is usually associated with a bachelor's degree or higher. **Exhibits 4, 8-11.**

Although a position need not qualify under all four criteria in this regulation, this position does. Therefore, we respectfully submit that the position of Research Chemist is a specialty occupation.

III.
BENEFICIARY IS QUALIFIED FOR THE POSITION OF RESEARCH CHEMIST.

The petitioner shall submit, along with an H-1B petition involving a specialty occupation, evidence that the alien qualifies to perform the services in the specialty occupation.[7] Although a four-year college degree is one way to qualify for a specialty occupation, the equivalent in relevant experience is another way to qualify.[8]

In the present case, Beneficiary is uniquely qualified for this position based upon his impressive academic achievements and experience. **Exhibits 2-4.**

Therefore, Beneficiary has the necessary qualifications for the current position.

IV.
PETITIONER SATISFIES ALL REQUIREMENTS.

The petitioner must be a "United States employer". The Code of Federal Regulations defines "United States employer" as follows:

> "United States employer means a person, firm, corporation, contractor, or other association, or organization in the United States which:
> (1) Engages a person to work within the United States;
> (2) Has an employer-employee relationship with respect to employees under this part, as indicated by the fact that it may hire, pay, fire, supervise, or otherwise control the work of any such employee; and
> (3) Has an Internal Revenue Service Tax identification number."

---

6 8 C.F.R. § 214.2(h)(4)(iii)(A)
7 8 C.F.R. § 214.2(h)(4)(iii)(B)(3)
8 8 C.F.R. § 214.2(h)(4)(iii)(C)(4)

8 C.F.R. § 214.2(h)(4)(I)(B)(2).

In the present case, Petitioner is in the United States; seeks to engage Beneficiary in an employer-employee relationship; would have the power to hire, pay, fire, supervise, or otherwise control the Beneficiary's work; and has an IRS tax identification number, as seen on the enclosed Form I-129. Therefore, Petitioner is an employer within the meaning of the regulations and is eligible to petition for an H-1B employee.

V.
LABOR CONDITION APPLICATION.

Prior to filing a petition with the U.S. Citizenship and Immigration Services (hereinafter "USCIS" or "Service") on behalf of an alien in a specialty occupation, the prospective employer must have filed a Labor Condition Application with the Department of Labor.[9]

In the present case, please see **Exhibit 7**.

VI.
CONCLUSION

For the forgoing reasons, Petitioner respectfully requests that the instant petition be approved and that Beneficiary's status be changed to from F-1 to H-1B.

If you should have any questions, please feel free to contact our office at (562) 495-0554.

Sincerely,

Brian D. Lerner
Attorney at Law

[9] 8 C.F.R. § 214.2(h)(1)(B)(1).

SECTION 2:
Forms

Form G-28: Notice of Entry of Appearance as Attorney or Accredited Representative (Petitioner)

Notice of Entry of Appearance as Attorney or Accredited Representative

Department of Homeland Security

DHS Form G-28
OMB No. 1615-0105
Expires 02/29/2016

Part 1. Information About Attorney or Accredited Representative

Name and Address of Attorney or Accredited Representative

1.a. Family Name *(Last Name)* Lerner

1.b. Given Name *(First Name)* [illegible]

1.c. Middle Name D

2. Name of Law Firm or Recognized Organization
Law Offices of Brian D Lerner

3. Name of Law Student or Law Graduate

4. State Bar Number 158536

5.a. Street Number 3233

5.b. Street Name E Broadway

5.c. Apt. [ ] Ste. [ ] Flr. [ ]

5.d. City or Town Long Beach

5.e. State CA 5.f. Zip Code 90803

5.g. Postal Code

5.h. Province

5.i. Country
U.S.A.

6. Daytime Phone Number (562) 495-0554

7. E-Mail Address of Attorney or Accredited Representative
blerner@californiaimmigration.us

Part 2. Eligibility Information For Attorney or Accredited Representative

(Check applicable items(s) below)

1. [X] I am an attorney eligible to practice law in, and a member in good standing of, the bar of the highest court(s) of the following State(s), possession(s), territory(ies), commonwealth(s), or the District of Columbia.

1.a. Supreme Court of California

1.b. I *(choose one)* [X] *am not* [ ] *am* subject to any order of any court or administrative agency disbarring, suspending, enjoining, restraining, or otherwise restricting me in the practice of law. (If you are subject to any order(s), explain fully in the space below.)

1.b.1.

2. [ ] I am an accredited representative of the following qualified nonprofit religious, charitable, social service, or similar organization established in the United States, so recognized by the Department of Justice, Board of Immigration Appeals pursuant to 8 CFR 292.2. Provide the name of the organization and the expiration date of accreditation.

2.a. Name of Recognized Organization

2.b. Date Accreditation expires *(mm/dd/yyyy)* ►

3. [ ] I am associated with

3.a.

the attorney or accredited representative of record who previously filed Form G-28 in this case, and my appearance as an attorney or accredited representative is at his or her request. If you check this item, also complete **number 1 (1.a. - 1.b.1.) or number 2 (2.a. - 2.b.) in Part 2** *(whichever is appropriate)*.

4. [ ] I am a law student or law graduate working under the direct supervision of the attorney or accredited representative of record on this form in accordance with the requirements in 8 CFR 292.1(a)(2)(iv).

Part 3. Notice of Appearance as Attorney or Accredited Representative

This appearance relates to immigration matters before (select one):

1. [X] USCIS - List the form number(s)

1.a. I-129

2. [ ] ICE - List the specific matter in which appearance is entered

2.a.

3. [ ] CBP - List the specific matter in which appearance is entered

3.a.

I hereby enter my appearance as attorney or accredited representative at the request of:

4. **Select only one:** [ ] Applicant [X] Petitioner [ ] Respondent (ICE, CBP)

Name of Applicant, Petitioner, or Respondent

5.a. Family Name *(Last Name)*

5.b. Given Name *(First Name)*

5.c. Middle Name

5.d. Name of Company or Organization, if applicable

Inland Empire Liver Foundation

NOTE: Provide the mailing address of Petitioner, Applicant, or Respondent and not the address of the attorney or accredited representative, except when a safe mailing address is permitted on an application or petition filed with Form G-28.

6.a. Street Number and Name 2006 N Riverside Avenue

6.b. Apt. [ ] Ste. [X] Flr. [ ] A

6.c. City or Town Rialto

6.d. State CA 6.e. Zip Code 92377

7. Provide A-Number and/or Receipt Number

Pursuant to the Privacy Act of 1974 and DHS policy, I hereby consent to the disclosure to the named Attorney or Accredited Representative of any record pertaining to me that appears in any system of records of USCIS, ICE, or CBP.

8.a. Signature of Applicant, Petitioner, or Respondent

8.b. Date *(mm/dd/yyyy)* ► 3.31.2015

Part 4. Signature of Attorney or Accredited Representative

I have read and understand the regulations and conditions contained in 8 CFR 103.2 and 292 governing appearances and representation before the Department of Homeland Security. I declare under penalty of perjury under the laws of the United States that the information I have provided on this form is true and correct.

1. Signature of Attorney or Accredited Representative

2. Signature of Law Student or Law Graduate

3. Date *(mm/dd/yyyy)* ► 3/31/2015

Part 5. Additional Information

1.

Form G-28: Notice of Entry of Appearance as Attorney or Accredited Representative (Beneficiary)

Notice of Entry of Appearance as Attorney or Accredited Representative

Department of Homeland Security

DHS Form G-28
OMB No. 1615-0105
Expires 02/29/2016

Part 1. Information About Attorney or Accredited Representative

Name and Address of Attorney or Accredited Representative

1.a. Family Name (Last Name): Lerner

1.b. Given Name (First Name): Brian

1.c. Middle Name: D

2. Name of Law Firm or Recognized Organization: Law Offices of Brian D Lerner

3. Name of Law Student or Law Graduate:

4. State Bar Number: 158536

5.a. Street Number: 3233

5.b. Street Name: E Broadway

5.c. Apt. [ ] Ste. [ ] Flr. [ ]

5.d. City or Town: Long Beach

5.e. State: CA 5.f. Zip Code: 90803

5.g. Postal Code:

5.h. Province:

5.i. Country: U.S.A.

6. Daytime Phone Number: (562) 495-0554

7. E-Mail Address of Attorney or Accredited Representative: blerner@californiaimmigration.us

Part 2. Eligibility Information For Attorney or Accredited Representative

(Check applicable items(s) below)

1. [X] I am an attorney eligible to practice law in, and a member in good standing of, the bar of the highest court(s) of the following State(s), possession(s), territory(ies), commonwealth(s), or the District of Columbia.

1.a. Supreme Court of California

1.b. I *(choose one)* [X] *am not* [ ] *am* subject to any order of any court or administrative agency disbarring, suspending, enjoining, restraining, or otherwise restricting me in the practice of law. (If you are subject to any order(s), explain fully in the space below.)

1.b.1.

2. [ ] I am an accredited representative of the following qualified nonprofit religious, charitable, social service, or similar organization established in the United States, so recognized by the Department of Justice, Board of Immigration Appeals pursuant to 8 CFR 292.2. Provide the name of the organization and the expiration date of accreditation.

2.a. Name of Recognized Organization

2.b. Date Accreditation expires *(mm/dd/yyyy)* ▶

3. [ ] I am associated with

3.a.

the attorney or accredited representative of record who previously filed Form G-28 in this case, and my appearance as an attorney or accredited representative is at his or her request. If you check this item, also complete **number 1 (1.a. - 1.b.1.) or number 2 (2.a. - 2.b.)** in **Part 2** *(whichever is appropriate)*.

4. [ ] I am a law student or law graduate working under the direct supervision of the attorney or accredited representative of record on this form in accordance with the requirements in 8 CFR 292.1(a)(2)(iv).

Part 3. Notice of Appearance as Attorney or Accredited Representative

This appearance relates to immigration matters before (select one):

1. [X] USCIS - List the form number(s)

1.a. I-129

2. [ ] ICE - List the specific matter in which appearance is entered

2.a.

3. [ ] CBP - List the specific matter in which appearance is entered

3.a.

I hereby enter my appearance as attorney or accredited representative at the request of:

4. **Select only one:** [X] Applicant [ ] Petitioner [ ] Respondent (ICE, CBP)

Name of Applicant, Petitioner, or Respondent

5.a. Family Name *(Last Name)* MUQAYAD

5.b. Given Name *(First Name)* Abdulmanem

5.c. Middle Name

5.d. Name of Company or Organization, if applicable

NOTE: Provide the mailing address of Petitioner, Applicant, or Respondent and not the address of the attorney or accredited representative, **except when a safe mailing address is permitted** on an application or petition filed with Form G-28.

6.a. Street Number and Name 2500 Harriman Lane

6.b. Apt. [ ] Ste. [ ] Flr. [ ]

6.c. City or Town Redondo Beach

6.d. State CA 6.e. Zip Code 90278

7. Provide A-Number and/or Receipt Number

206 859 896

Pursuant to the Privacy Act of 1974 and DHS policy, I hereby consent to the disclosure to the named Attorney or Accredited Representative of any record pertaining to me that appears in any system of records of USCIS, ICE, or CBP.

8.a. Signature of Applicant, Petitioner, or Respondent

[signature]

8.b. Date *(mm/dd/yyyy)* ► 03/31/2015

Part 4. Signature of Attorney or Accredited Representative

I have read and understand the regulations and conditions contained in 8 CFR 103.2 and 292 governing appearances and representation before the Department of Homeland Security. I declare under penalty of perjury under the laws of the United States that the information I have provided on this form is true and correct.

1. Signature of Attorney or Accredited Representative

[signature]

2. Signature of Law Student or Law Graduate

3. Date *(mm/dd/yyyy)* ► 3/31/2015

Part 5. Additional Information

1.

Form I-129: Petition for a Nonimmigrant Worker

Petition for a Nonimmigrant Worker

Department of Homeland Security
U.S. Citizenship and Immigration Services

USCIS
Form I-129
OMB No. 1615-0009
Expires 10/31/2016

For USCIS Use Only	Receipt	Partial Approval *(explain)*	Action Block

Class:
No. of Workers:
Job Code:
Validity Dates:
From:
To:

☐ Classification Approved
☐ Consulate/POE/PFI Notified
At:
☐ Extension Granted
☐ COS/Extension Granted

► **START HERE - Type or print in black ink.**

Part 1. Petitioner Information

If you are an individual filing this petition, complete **Item Number 1. If you are a company or an organization filing this petition,** complete **Item Number 2.**

1. Legal Name of Individual Petitioner

Family Name *(last name)* | Given Name *(first name)* | Middle Name

2. Company or Organization Name

Inland Empire Liver Foundation

3. Mailing Address of Individual, Company or Organization

In Care Of Name

Apt. Ste. Flr. Number
☐ ☒ ☐ A

City or Town: Ri al to
State: CA
ZIP Code: 92377

Province
Postal Code
Country: USA

4. Contact Information

Daytime Telephone Number: (909) 883-2999
Mobile Telephone Number
E-mail Address *(if any)*

5. Other Information

Federal Employer Identification Number (FEIN): ► 45-4165908
Individual IRS Tax Number: ►
U.S. Social Security Number *(if any)*: ►

Part 2. Information About This Petition *(See instructions for fee information)*

1. **Requested Nonimmigrant Classification** *(Write classification symbol)*: H-1B

2. **Basis for Classification** *(select only one box)*:
   - ☒ a. New employment.
   - ☐ b. Continuation of previously approved employment without change with the same employer.
   - ☐ c. Change in previously approved employment.
   - ☐ d. New concurrent employment.
   - ☐ e. Change of employer.
   - ☐ f. Amended petition.

3. **Provide the most recent petition/application receipt number for the beneficiary. If none exists, indicate "None."** ►

4. **Requested Action** *(select only one box)*:
   - ☐ a. Notify the office in Part 4 so each beneficiary can obtain a visa or be admitted. (**NOTE:** *A petition is not required for E-1, E-2, E-3, H-1B1 Chile/Singapore, or TN visa beneficiaries.*)
   - ☒ b. Change the status and extend the stay of each beneficiary because the beneficiary(ies) is/are now in the United States in another status (see instructions for limitations). This is available only when you check "New Employment" in **Item Number 2.**, above.
   - ☐ c. Extend the stay of each beneficiary because the beneficiary(ies) now hold(s) this status.
   - ☐ d. Amend the stay of each beneficiary because the beneficiary(ies) now hold(s) this status.
   - ☐ e. Extend the status of a nonimmigrant classification based on a free trade agreement. (See Trade Agreement Supplement to Form I-129 for TN and H-1B1.)
   - ☐ f. Change status to a nonimmigrant classification based on a free trade agreement. (See Trade Agreement Supplement to Form I-129 for TN and H-1B1.)

5. **Total number of workers included in this petition.** *(See instructions relating to when more than one worker can be included.)* ► 1

Part 3. Beneficiary Information *(Information about the beneficiary/beneficiaries you are filing for. Complete the blocks below. Use the Attachment-1 sheet to name each beneficiary included in this petition.)*

1. **If an Entertainment Group, Provide the Group Name**

2. **Provide Name of Beneficiary**

Family Name *(last name)*	Given Name *(first name)*	Middle Name

3. **Provide all other names the beneficiary has used.** Include nicknames, aliases, maiden name, and names from all previous marriages.

Family Name *(last name)*	Given Name *(first name)*	Middle Name
N/A		

4. **Other Information**

Date of birth *(mm/dd/yyyy)* ► 04/12/1976   Gender ☒ Male ☐ Female   U.S. Social Security Number *(if any)* ► N/A

Part 3. Beneficiary Information (Information about the beneficiary/beneficiaries you are filing for. *Complete the blocks below. Use the Attachment-1 sheet to name each beneficiary included in this petition.) (continued)*

Alien Registration Number (A-Number): ► A- 206-859-896

Country of Birth: Syr ia

Province of Birth:

Country of Citizenship or Nationality: Syria

5. **If the beneficiary is in the United States, complete the following:**

Date of Last Arrival *(mm/dd/yyyy)*: 01/09/2014

I-94 Arrival-Departure Record Number: ►

Passport or Travel Document Number:

Date Passport or Travel Document Issued *(mm/dd/yyyy)*: 03/01/2009

Date Passport or Travel Document Expires *(mm/dd/yyyy)*: 02/28/2015

Passport or Travel Document Country of Issuance: Syria

Current Nonimmigrant Status: F-1

Date Status Expires *or D/S* *(mm/dd/yyyy)* ► 03/30/2016

Student and Exchange Visitor Information System (SEVIS) Number *(if any)*:

Employment Authorization Document (EAD) Number *(if any)*:

6. **Current Residential U.S. Address** *(if applicable) (do not list a P.O. Box)*

Street Number and Name: 2500 Harriman Lane

Apt. Ste. Flr. ☐ ☐ ☐ Number:

City or Town: Redondo Beach

State: CA

ZIP Code: 90278

Part 4. Processing Information

1. If a beneficiary or beneficiaries named in Part 3. is/are outside the United States, or a requested extension of stay or change of status cannot be granted, state the U.S. Consulate or inspection facility you want notified if this petition is approved.

a. **Type of Office** *(select only one box)*: ☒ Consulate ☐ Pre-flight inspection ☐ Port of Entry

b. **Office Address** *(City)*: Damascus

c. **U.S. State or Foreign Country**: Syria

d. **Beneficiary's Foreign Address**

Street Number and Name:

Apt. Ste. Flr. ☐ ☐ ☐ Number:

City or Town: Al ep po

State:

Province:

Postal Code:

Country: Syria

2. Does each person in this petition have a valid passport? ☐ Yes ☒ No. If no, go to Part 9. and type or print your explanation.

Part 4. Processing Information *(continued)*

3. Are you filing any other petitions with this one?
☐ Yes. If yes, how many? ▶ ☒ No

4. Are you filing any applications for replacement/initial I-94, Arrival-Departure Records with this petition? Note that if the beneficiary was issued an electronic Form I-94 by CBP when he/she was admitted to the United States at an air or sea port, he/she may be able to obtain the Form I-94 from the CBP Web site at **www.cbp.gov/i94** instead of filing an application for a replacement/initial I-94.
☐ Yes. If yes, how many? ▶ ☒ No

5. Are you filing any applications for dependents with this petition?
☐ Yes. If yes, how many? ▶ ☒ No

6. Is any beneficiary in this petition in removal proceedings?
☐ Yes. If yes, proceed to **Part 9.** and list the beneficiary's(ies) name(s). ☒ No

7. Have you ever filed an immigrant petition for any beneficiary in this petition?
☐ Yes. If yes, how many? ▶ ☒ No

8. Did you indicate you were filing a new petition in **Part 2.**?
☒ Yes. If yes, answer the questions below. ☐ No. If no, proceed to **Item Number 9.**

a. Has any beneficiary in this petition ever been given the classification you are now requesting within the last 7 years?
☐ Yes. If yes, proceed to **Part 9.** and type or print your explanation. ☒ No

b. Has any beneficiary in this petition ever been denied the classification you are now requesting within the last 7 years?
☐ Yes. If yes, proceed to **Part 9.** and type or print your explanation. ☒ No

9. Have you ever previously filed a nonimmigrant petition for this beneficiary?
☐ Yes. If yes, proceed to **Part 9.** and type or print your explanation. ☒ No

10. If you are filing for an entertainment group, has any beneficiary in this petition not been with the group for at least 1 year?
☐ Yes. If yes, proceed to **Part 9.** and type or print your explanation. ☒ No

11.a. Has any beneficiary in this petition ever been a J-1 exchange visitor or J-2 dependent of a J-1 exchange visitor?
☐ Yes. If yes, proceed to **Item Number 11.b.** ☒ No

11.b. If you checked yes in **Item Number 11.a.**, provide the dates the beneficiary maintained status as a J-1 exchange visitor or J-2 dependent. Also, provide evidence of this status by attaching a copy of either a DS-2019, Certificate of Eligibility for Exchange Visitor (J-1) Status, a Form IAP-66, or a copy of the passport that includes the J visa stamp.

Part 5. Basic Information About the Proposed Employment and Employer

Attach the Form I-129 supplement relevant to the classification of the worker(s) you are requesting.

1. Job Title: Research Chemist
2. LCA or ETA Case Number:

Part 5. Basic Information About the Proposed Employment and Employer *(continued)*

3. Address where the beneficiary(ies) will work if different from address in **Part 1**.

Street Number and Name	Apt. Ste. Flr.	Number
	☐ ☒ ☐	A

City or Town	State	ZIP Code
Ri al to	CA	92377

4. Did you include an itinerary with the petition? ☐ Yes ☒ No

5. Will the beneficiary(ies) work for you off-site at another company or organization's location? ☐ Yes ☒ No

6. Will the beneficiary(ies) work exclusively in the Commonwealth of the Northern Mariana Islands (CNMI)? ☐ Yes ☒ No

7. Is this a full-time position? ☐ Yes ☒ No

8. If the answer to **Item Number 7.** is no, how many hours per week for the position? ► 15

9. Wages: $ 30.95 per *(Specify hour, week, month, or year)* ► Hour

10. Other Compensation *(Explain)*

N/A

11. Dates of intended employment From: *(mm/dd/yyyy)* ► 10/01/2015 To: *(mm/dd/yyyy)* ► 09/29/2018

12. Type of Business: Not for Profit Health Care Organization

13. Year Established: 2011

14. Current Number of Employees in the United States: 7

15. Gross Annual Income:

16. Net Annual Income:

Part 6. Certification Regarding the Release of Controlled Technology or Technical Data to Foreign Persons in the United States

(This section of the form is required only for H-1B, H-1B1 Chile/Singapore, L-1, and O-1A petitions. It is not required for any other classifications. Please review the Form I-129 General Filing Instructions before completing this section.)

Select Item Number 1. or Item Number 2. as appropriate. DO NOT select both boxes.

With respect to the technology or technical data the petitioner will release or otherwise provide access to the beneficiary, the petitioner certifies that it has reviewed the Export Administration Regulations (EAR) and the International Traffic in Arms Regulations (ITAR) and has determined that:

1. ☒ A license is not required from either the U.S. Department of Commerce or the U.S. Department of State to release such technology or technical data to the foreign person; or

2. ☐ A license is required from the U.S. Department of Commerce and/or the U.S. Department of State to release such technology or technical data to the beneficiary and the petitioner will prevent access to the controlled technology or technical data by the beneficiary until and unless the petitioner has received the required license or other authorization to release it to the beneficiary.

Part 7. Signature and Contact Information of Authorized Signatory *(Read the information on penalties in the instructions before completing this section.)*

I certify, under penalty of perjury, that this petition and the evidence submitted with it are true and correct to the best of my knowledge. Copies of documents submitted are exact photocopies of unaltered original documents, and I understand that, as a petitioner, I may be required to submit original documents to U.S. Citizenship and Immigration Services (USCIS) at a later date. I authorize the release of any information from my records, or from the petitioning organization's records that USCIS needs to determine eligibility for the benefit being sought. I recognize the authority of USCIS to conduct audits of this petition using publicly available open source information. I also recognize that supporting evidence submitted may be verified by USCIS through any means determined appropriate by USCIS, including but not limited to, on-site compliance reviews.

1. **Name and Title of Authorized Signatory**

Family Name *(last name)*:

Given Name *(first name)*:

Title: President

2. **Signature and Date**

Signature of Authorized Signatory: [signature]

Date of Signature *(mm/dd/yyyy)* ▶ 3/31/2015

3. **Signatory's Contact Information**

Daytime Telephone Number: (909) 883-2099

E-mail Address *(if any)*:

NOTE: *If you do not fully complete this form or fail to submit the required documents listed in the instructions, a final decision on your petition may be delayed or the petition may be denied.*

Part 8. Declaration, Signature, and Contact Information of Person Preparing Form, If Other Than Above

Provide the following information concerning the preparer:

1. **Name of Preparer**

Family Name *(last name)*: Lerner

Given Name *(first name)*: Brian

2. **Preparer's Business or Organization Name**

(If applicable, provide the name of your accredited organization recognized by the Board of Immigration Appeals (BIA).)

Law Offices of Brian D. Lerner, APC

3. **Preparer's Mailing Address**

Street Number and Name: 3233 E. Broadway

Apt. Ste. Flr. Number:

City or Town: LLong Beach

State: CA

ZIP Code: 90803

Province:

Postal Code:

Country: USA

4. **Preparer's Contact Information**

Daytime Telephone Number: (562) 495-0554

Fax Number: (323) 400-4236

E-mail Address *(if any)*: blerner@californiaimmigration.us

Part 8. Declaration, Signature, and Contact Information of Person Preparing Form, If Other Than Above *(continued)*

Preparer's Declaration

By my signature, I certify, swear or affirm, under penalty of perjury, that I prepared this form on behalf of, at the request of, and with the express consent of, the petitioner. I completed the form based only on responses the petitioner provided to me. After completing the form, I reviewed it and all of the petitioner's responses with the petitioner, who agreed with every answer provided for every question on the form and, when required, supplied additional information to respond to a question on the form.

5. **Signature and Date**

Signature of Preparer: [signature]

Date of Signature *(mm/dd/yyyy)* ► 3/31/2015

Part 9. Additional Information About Your Petition For Nonimmigrant Worker

If you require more space to provide any additional information within this petition, use the space below. If you require more space than what is provided to complete this petition, you may make a copy of **Part 9.** to complete and file with this petition. In order to assist us in reviewing your response, you must identify the **Page Number, Part Number and Item Number** corresponding to the additional information.

1. A-Number ▶

2. **Page Number** 3 **Part Number** 4 **Item Number** 2

Beneficiary has applied to renew his passport.

3. **Page Number** **Part Number** **Item Number**

4. **Page Number** **Part Number** **Item Number**

5. Signature and Date

Petitioner's Signature

Date of Signature (mm/dd/yyyy) ▶ 3/31/2015

Form I-120:
H Classification Supplement to Form I-129

H Classification Supplement to Form I-129

Department of Homeland Security
U.S. Citizenship and Immigration Services

USCIS
Form I-129
OMB No. 1615-0009
Expires 10/31/2016

1. Name of the Petitioner

Inland Empire Liver Foundation

Name of the beneficiary or if this petition includes multiple beneficiaries, the total number of beneficiaries

2.a. Name of the Beneficiary

OR

2.b. Provide the total number of beneficiaries

3. List each beneficiary's prior periods of stay in H or L classification in the United States for the last 6 years (beneficiaries requesting H-2A or H-2B classification need only list the last 3 years). Be sure to only list those periods in which each beneficiary was actually in the United States in an H or L classification. Do not include periods in which the beneficiary was in a dependent status, for example, H-4 or L-2 status.

NOTE: Submit photocopies of Forms I-94, I-797, and/or other USCIS issued documents noting these periods of stay in the H or L classification. *(If more space is needed, attach an additional sheet.)*

Subject's Name	Period of Stay *(mm/dd/yyyy)* From	To

4. Classification sought *(select only one box)*:

☒ a. H-1B Specialty Occupation

☐ b. H-1B1 Chile and Singapore

☐ c. H-1B2 Exceptional services relating to a cooperative research and development project administered by the U.S. Department of Defense (DOD)

☐ d. H-1B3 Fashion model of distinguished merit and ability

☐ e. H-2A Agricultural worker

☐ f. H-2B Non-agricultural worker

☐ g. H-3 Trainee

☐ h. H-3 Special education exchange visitor program

5. Are you filing this petition on behalf of a beneficiary subject to the Guam-CNMI cap exemption under Public Law 110-229?

☐ Yes ☒ No

6. Are you requesting a change of employer and was the beneficiary previously subject to the Guam-CNMI cap exemption under Public Law 110-229?

☐ Yes ☒ No

7.a. Does any beneficiary in this petition have ownership interest in the petitioning organization?

☐ Yes. If yes, please explain in **Item Number 7.b.** ☒ No

7.b. Explanation

Section 1. Complete This Section If Filing for H-1B Classification

1. Describe the proposed duties.

   See Attached.

2. Describe the beneficiary's present occupation and summary of prior work experience.

   Present Occupation: F-1
   Work Experience: Pharmacist/Doctor - see attached.

Statement for H-1B Specialty Occupations and H-1B1 Chile and Singapore

By filing this petition, I agree to, and will abide by, the terms of the labor condition application (LCA) for the duration of the beneficiary's authorized period of stay for H-1B employment. I certify that I will maintain a valid employer-employee relationship with the beneficiary at all times. If the beneficiary is assigned to a position in a new location, I will obtain and post an LCA for that site prior to reassignment.

I further understand that I cannot charge the beneficiary the ACWIA fee, and that any other required reimbursement will be considered an offset against wages and benefits paid relative to the LCA.

Signature of Petitioner	Name of Petitioner	Date (mm/dd/yyyy)
		3/31/2015

Statement for H-1B Specialty Occupations and U.S. Department of Defense (DOD) Projects

As an authorized official of the employer, I certify that the employer will be liable for the reasonable costs of return transportation of the alien abroad if the beneficiary is dismissed from employment by the employer before the end of the period of authorized stay.

Signature of Authorized Official of Employer	Name of Authorized Official of Employer	Date (mm/dd/yyyy)
		3/31/2015

Statement for H-1B U.S. Department of Defense Projects Only

I certify that the beneficiary will be working on a cooperative research and development project or a co-production project under a reciprocal government-to-government agreement administered by the U.S. Department of Defense.

Signature of DOD Project Manager	Name of DOD Project Manager	Date (mm/dd/yyyy)

Section 2. Complete This Section If Filing for H-2A or H-2B Classification

1. Employment is: *(select only one box)*

   ☐ a. Seasonal ☐ b. Peak load ☐ c. Intermittent ☐ d. One-time occurrence

2. Temporary need is: *(select only one box)*

   ☐ a. Unpredictable ☐ b. Periodic ☐ c. Recurrent annually

Section 2. Complete This Section If Filing for H-2A or H-2B Classification *(continued)*

3. Explain your temporary need for the workers' services *(Attach a separate sheet if additional space is needed).*

4. List the countries of citizenship for the H-2A or H-2B workers you plan to hire.

a.	d.
b.	e.
c.	f.

5.a. You must provide all of the requested information for **Item Numbers 5.a. - 6.** for each H-2A or H-2B worker you plan to hire who is not from a country that has been designated as a participating country in accordance with 8 CFR 214.2(h)(5)(i)(F)(1) or 214.2(h)(6)(i)(E)(1). See www.uscis.gov for the list of participating countries. *(Attach a separate sheet if additional space is needed.)*

Family Name *(last name)* Given Name *(first name)* Middle Name

5.b. Provide all other name(s) used

Family Name *(last name)* Given Name *(first name)* Middle Name

5.c. Date of Birth *(mm/dd/yyyy)* 5.d. Country of Birth

5.e. Country of Citizenship or Nationality

6.a. Have any of the workers listed in **Item Number 5** above ever been admitted to the United States previously in H-2A/H-2B status?

☐ Yes. If yes, go to **Part 9.** of Form I-129 and write your explanation. ☐ No

6.b. Visa Classification (H-2A or H-2B):

NOTE: If any of the H-2A or H-2B workers you are requesting are nationals of a country that is not on the eligible countries list, you must also provide evidence showing: (1) that workers with the required skills are not available from a country currently on the eligible countries list*; (2) whether the beneficiaries have been admitted previously to the United States in H-2A or H-2B status; (3) that there is no potential for abuse, fraud, or other harm to the integrity of the H-2A or H-2B visa programs through the potential admission of the intended workers; and (4) any other factors that may serve the United States interest.

* For H-2A petitions only: You must also show that workers with the required skills are not available from among United States workers.

7.a. Did you or do you plan to use a staffing, recruiting, or similar placement service or agent to locate the H-2A/H-2B workers that you intend to hire by filing this petition?

☐ Yes ☐ No

If yes, list the name and address of service or agent used below. Please use **Part 9.** of Form I-129 if you need to include the name and address of more than one service or agent.

7.b. Name

Section 2. Complete This Section If Filing for H-2A or H-2B Classification *(continued)*

7.c. Address

Street Number and Name | Apt. Ste. Flr. Number

City or Town | State | ZIP Code

8.a. Did any of the H-2A/H-2B workers that you are requesting pay you, or an agent, a job placement fee or other form of compensation (either direct or indirect) as a condition of the employment, or do they have an agreement to pay you or the service such fees at a later date? The phrase "fees or other compensation" includes, but is not limited to, petition fees, attorney fees, recruitment costs, and any other fees that are a condition of a beneficiary's employment that the employer is prohibited from passing to the H-2A or H-2B worker under law under U.S. Department of Labor rules. This phrase does not include reasonable travel expenses and certain government-mandated fees (such as passport fees) that are not prohibited from being passed to the H-2A or H-2B worker by statute, regulations, or any laws. ☐ Yes ☐ No

8.b. If yes, list the types and amounts of fees that the worker(s) paid or will pay.

8.c. If the workers paid any fee or compensation, were they reimbursed? ☐ Yes ☐ No

8.d. If the workers agreed to pay a fee that they have not yet been paid, has their agreement been terminated before the workers paid the fee? *(Submit evidence of termination or reimbursement with this petition.)* ☐ Yes ☐ No

9. Have you made reasonable inquiries to determine that to the best of your knowledge the recruiter, facilitator, or similar employment service that you used has not collected, and will not collect, directly or indirectly, any fees or other compensation from the H-2 workers of this petition as a condition of the H-2 workers' employment? ☐ Yes ☐ No

NOTE: If USCIS determines that you knew, or should have known, that the workers requested in connection with this petition paid any fees or other compensation at any time as a condition of employment, your petition may be denied or revoked. ☐ Yes ☐ No

10.a. Have you ever had an H-2A or H-2B petition denied or revoked because an employee paid a job placement fee or other similar compensation as a condition of the job offer or employment? ☐ Yes ☐ No

10.a.1 If yes, when?

10.a.2 Receipt Number: ►

10.b. Were the workers reimbursed for such fees and compensation? (Submit evidence of reimbursement.) If you answered no because you were unable to locate the workers, include evidence of your efforts to locate the workers. ☐ Yes ☐ No

11. Have any of the workers you are requesting experienced an interrupted stay associated with their entry as an H-2A or H-2B? *(See form instructions for more information on interrupted stays.)* ☐ Yes ☐ No

If yes, document the workers' periods of stay in the table on the first page of this supplement. Submit evidence of each entry and each exit, with the petition, as evidence of the interrupted stays.

12.a. If you are an H-2A petitioner, are you a participant in the E-Verify program? ☐ Yes ☐ No

12.b. If yes, provide the E-Verify Company ID or Client Company ID.

Section 2. Complete This Section If Filing for H-2A or H-2B Classification *(continued)*

The H-2A/H-2B petitioner and each employer consent to allow Government access to the site where the labor is being performed for the purpose of determining compliance with H-2A/H-2B requirements. The petitioner further agrees to notify DHS beginning on a date and in a manner specified in a notice published in the Federal Register within 2 workdays if: an H-2A/H-2B worker fails to report for work within 5 workdays after the employment start date stated on the petition or, applicable to H-2A petitioners only, within 5 workdays of the start date established by the petitioner, whichever is later; the agricultural labor or services for which H-2A/H-2B workers were hired is completed more than 30 days early; or the H-2A/H-2B worker absconds from the worksite or is terminated prior to the completion of agricultural labor or services for which he or she was hired. The petitioner agrees to retain evidence of such notification and make it available for inspection by DHS officers for a 1-year period. "Workday" means the period between the time on any particular day when such employee commences his or her principal activity and the time on that day at which he or she ceases such principal activity or activities.

For H-2A petitioners only: The petitioner agrees to pay $10 in liquidated damages for each instance where it cannot demonstrate it is in compliance with the notification requirement.

The petitioner must execute **Part A**. If the petitioner is the employer's agent, the employer must execute **Part B**. If there are joint employers, they must each execute **Part C**.

Part A. Petitioner

By filing this petition, I agree to the conditions of H-2A/H-2B employment and agree to the notification requirements. For H-2A petitioners: I also agree to the liquidated damages requirements defined in 8 CFR 214.2(h)(5)(vi)(B)(3).

Signature of Petitioner	**Name of Petitioner**	**Date** *(mm/dd/yyyy)*

Part B. Employer who is not the petitioner

I certify that I have authorized the party filing this petition to act as my agent in this regard. I assume full responsibility for all representations made by this agent on my behalf and agree to the conditions of H-2A/H-2B eligibility.

Signature of Employer	**Name of Employer**	**Date** *(mm/dd/yyyy)*

Part C. Joint Employers

I agree to the conditions of H-2A eligibility.

Signature of Joint Employer	**Name of Joint Employer**	**Date** *(mm/dd/yyyy)*
Signature of Joint Employer	**Name of Joint Employer**	**Date** *(mm/dd/yyyy)*
Signature of Joint Employer	**Name of Joint Employer**	**Date** *(mm/dd/yyyy)*
Signature of Joint Employer	**Name of Joint Employer**	**Date** *(mm/dd/yyyy)*

Section 3. Complete This Section If Filing for H-3 Classification

If you answer yes to any of the following questions, attach a full explanation.

1. Is the training you intend to provide, or similar training, available in the beneficiary's country? ☐ Yes ☐ No
2. Will the training benefit the beneficiary in pursuing a career abroad? ☐ Yes ☐ No
3. Does the training involve productive employment incidental to the training? If yes, explain the amount of compensation employment versus the classroom in **Part 9. of Form I-129.** ☐ Yes ☐ No
4. Does the beneficiary already have skills related to the training? ☐ Yes ☐ No
5. Is this training an effort to overcome a labor shortage? ☐ Yes ☐ No
6. Do you intend to employ the beneficiary abroad at the end of this training? ☐ Yes ☐ No
7. If you do not intend to employ the beneficiary abroad at the end of this training, explain why you wish to incur the cost of providing this training and your expected return from this training.

Form I-129: H-1B and H-1B1 Data Collection and Filing Fee Exemption Supplement

H-1B and H-1B1 Data Collection and Filing Fee Exemption Supplement

Department of Homeland Security
U.S. Citizenship and Immigration Services

USCIS
Form I-129
OMB No. 1615-0009
Expires 10/31/2016

1. Name of the Petitioner
Inland Empire Liver Foundation

2. Name of the Beneficiary

Section 1. General Information

1. **Employer Information** - *(check all items that apply)*
   - a. Is the petitioner an H-1B dependent employer? ☐ Yes ☒ No
   - b. Has the petitioner ever been found to be a willful violator? ☐ Yes ☒ No
   - c. Is the beneficiary an H-1B nonimmigrant exempt from the Department of Labor attestation requirements? ☐ Yes ☒ No
     - c.1. If yes, is it because the beneficiary's annual rate of pay is equal to at least $60,000? ☐ Yes ☐ No
     - c.2. Or is it because the beneficiary has a master's degree or higher degree in a specialty related to the employment? ☐ Yes ☐ No
   - d. Does the petitioner employ 50 or more individuals in the United States? ☐ Yes ☒ No
     - d.1. If yes, are more than 50 percent of those employees in H-1B or L-1A or L-1B nonimmigrant status? ☐ Yes ☐ No

2. **Beneficiary's Highest Level of Education** *(select only one box)*
   - ☐ a. NO DIPLOMA
   - ☐ b. HIGH SCHOOL GRADUATE DIPLOMA or the equivalent (example: GED)
   - ☐ c. Some college credit, but less than 1 year
   - ☐ d. One or more years of college, no degree
   - ☐ e. Associate's degree *(for example: AA, AS)*
   - ☒ f. Bachelor's degree *(for example: BA, AB, BS)*
   - ☐ g. Master's degree *(for example: MA, MS, MEng, MEd, MSW, MBA)*
   - ☐ h. Professional degree *(for example: MD, DDS, DVM, LLB, JD)*
   - ☐ i. Doctorate degree *(for example: PhD, EdD)*

3. Major/Primary Field of Study
Pharmacy and Pharmaceutical Chemistry

4. Rate of Pay Per Year
$24,141

5. DOT Code

6. NAICS Code
1 9 2 0 3 1

Section 2. Fee Exemption and/or Determination

In order for USCIS to determine if you must pay the additional $1,500 or $750 American Competitiveness and Workforce Improvement Act (ACWIA) fee, answer all of the following questions:

1. Are you an institution of higher education as defined in section 101(a) of the Higher Education Act of 1965, 20 U.S.C. 1001(a)? ☐ Yes ☒ No
2. Are you a nonprofit organization or entity related to or affiliated with an institution of higher education, as defined in section 101(a) of the Higher Education Act of 1965, 20 U.S.C. 1001(a)? ☐ Yes ☒ No

Section 2. Fee Exemption and/or Determination *(continued)*

3. Are you a nonprofit research organization or a governmental research organization, as defined in 8 CFR 214.2(h)(19)(iii)(C)? ☐ Yes ☒ No

4. Is this the second or subsequent request for an extension of stay that this petitioner has filed for this alien? ☐ Yes ☒ No

5. Is this an amended petition that does not contain any request for extensions of stay? ☐ Yes ☒ No

6. Are you filing this petition to correct a USCIS error? ☐ Yes ☒ No

7. Is the petitioner a primary or secondary education institution? ☐ Yes ☒ No

8. Is the petitioner a nonprofit entity that engages in an established curriculum-related clinical training of students registered at such an institution? ☐ Yes ☒ No

If you answered yes to any of the questions above, you are not required to submit the ACWIA fee for your H-1B Form I-129 petition. If you answered no to all questions, answer **Item Number 9.** below.

9. Do you currently employ a total of 25 or fewer full-time equivalent employees in the United States, including all affiliates or subsidiaries of this company/organization? ☒ Yes ☐ No

If you answered yes, to **Item Number** 9. above, you are required to pay an additional ACWIA fee of **$750**. If you answered no, then you are required to pay an additional ACWIA fee of **$1,500**.

NOTE: A petitioner seeking initial approval of H-1B nonimmigrant status for a beneficiary, or seeking approval to employ an H-1B nonimmigrant currently working for another employer, must submit an additional **$500** Fraud Prevention and Detection fee. For petitions filed before October 1, 2015, an additional fee of **$2,000** must be submitted if you responded yes to **Item Numbers 1.d. and 1.d.1. of Section 1** of this supplement. This **$2,000** fee was mandated by the provisions of Public Law 111-230, as amended by Public Law 111-347.

The Fraud Prevention and Detection Fee and the Public Law 111-230 fee do not apply to H-1B1 petitions. **These fees, when applicable, may not be waived.** You must include payment of the fee(s) when you submit this form. Failure to submit the fee(s) when required will result in rejection or denial of your submission. *Each of these fee(s) should be paid by separate check(s) or money order(s).*

Section 3. Numerical Limitation Information

1. Specify the type of H-1B petition you are filing. *(select only one box)*:

   ☒ a. CAP H-1B Bachelor's Degree ☐ c. CAP H-1B1 Chile/Singapore

   ☐ b. CAP H-1B U.S. Master's Degree or Higher ☐ d. CAP Exempt

2. If you answered **Item Number 1.b. "CAP H-1B U.S. Master's Degree or Higher,"** provide the following information regarding the master's or higher degree the beneficiary has earned from a U.S. institution as defined in 20 U.S.C. 1001(a):

   a. Name of the United States institution of higher education

   b. Date Degree Awarded c. Type of United States Degree

   d. Address of the United States institution of higher education

   Street Number and Name Apt. Ste. Flr. Number

   City or Town State ZIP Code

Section 3. Numerical Limitation Information *(continued)*

3. If you answered **Item Number 1.d. "CAP Exempt,"** you must specify the reason(s) this petition is exempt from the numerical limitation for H-1B classification:

☐ **a.** The petitioner is an institution of higher education as defined in section 101(a) of the Higher Education Act, of 1965, 20 U.S.C. 1001(a).

☐ **b.** The petitioner is a nonprofit entity related to or affiliated with an institution of higher education as defined in section 101(a) of the Higher Education Act of 1965, 20 U.S.C. 1001(a).

☐ **c.** The petitioner is a nonprofit research organization or a governmental research organization as defined in 8 CFR 214.2(h)(19)(iii)(C).

☐ **d.** The petitioner will employ the beneficiary to perform job duties at a qualifying institution (see **Item Numbers 3.a. - 3.c.** above) that directly and predominately furthers the normal, primary, or essential purpose, mission, objectives, or function of the qualifying institution, namely higher education or nonprofit or government research.

☐ **e.** The petitioner is requesting an amendment to or extension of stay for the beneficiary's current H-1B classification.

☐ **f.** The beneficiary of this petition is a J-1 nonimmigrant physician who has received a waiver based on section 214(l) of the Act.

☐ **g.** The beneficiary of this petition has been counted against the cap and: **(1)** was previously granted status as an H-1B nonimmigrant in the past 6 years, **(2)** is applying from abroad to reclaim the remaining portion of the 6 years, or **(3)** is seeking an extension beyond the 6 year limitation based upon sections 104(c) or 106(a) of the American Competitiveness in the Twenty-First Century Act (AC21).

☐ **h.** The petitioner is an employer subject to the Guam-CNMI cap exemption pursuant to Public Law 110-229.

Section 4. Off-Site Assignment of H-1B Beneficiaries

1. The beneficiary of this petition will be assigned to work at an off-site location for all or part of the period for which H-1B classification sought. ☐ Yes ☒ No

   If no, do not complete **Item Numbers 2.** and **3.**

2. Placement of the beneficiary off-site during the period of employment will comply with the statutory and regulatory requirements of the H-1B nonimmigrant classification. ☐ Yes ☐ No

3. The beneficiary will be paid the higher of the prevailing or actual wage at any and all off-site locations. ☐ Yes ☐ No

SECTION 3:
Exhibits

Beneficiary's Passport and I-94

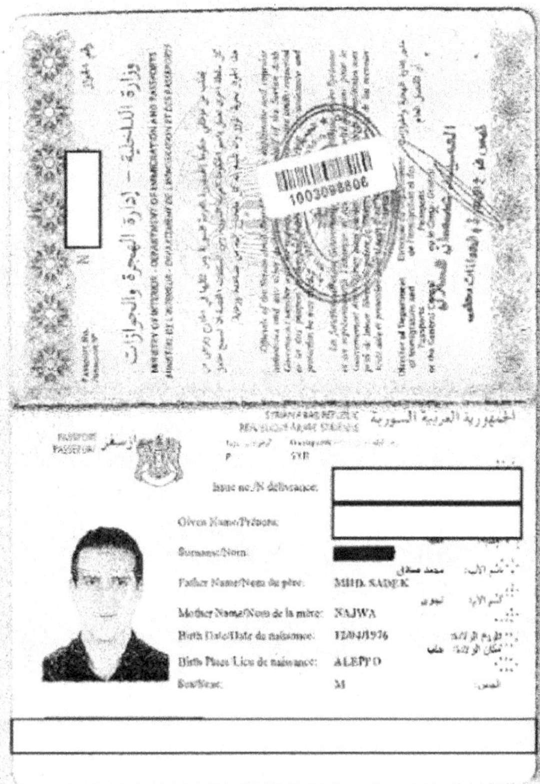
الجمهورية العربية السورية
SYRIAN ARAB REPUBLIC
PASSPORT
PASSEPORT
جواز سفر
P
SYR
Issue no./N délivrance:
Given Name/Prénom:
Surname/Nom:
Father Name/Nom du père: MHD. SADEK
Mother Name/Nom de la mère: NAJWA
Birth Date/Date de naissance: 12/04/1976
Birth Place/Lieu de naissance: ALEPPO
Sex/Sexe: M

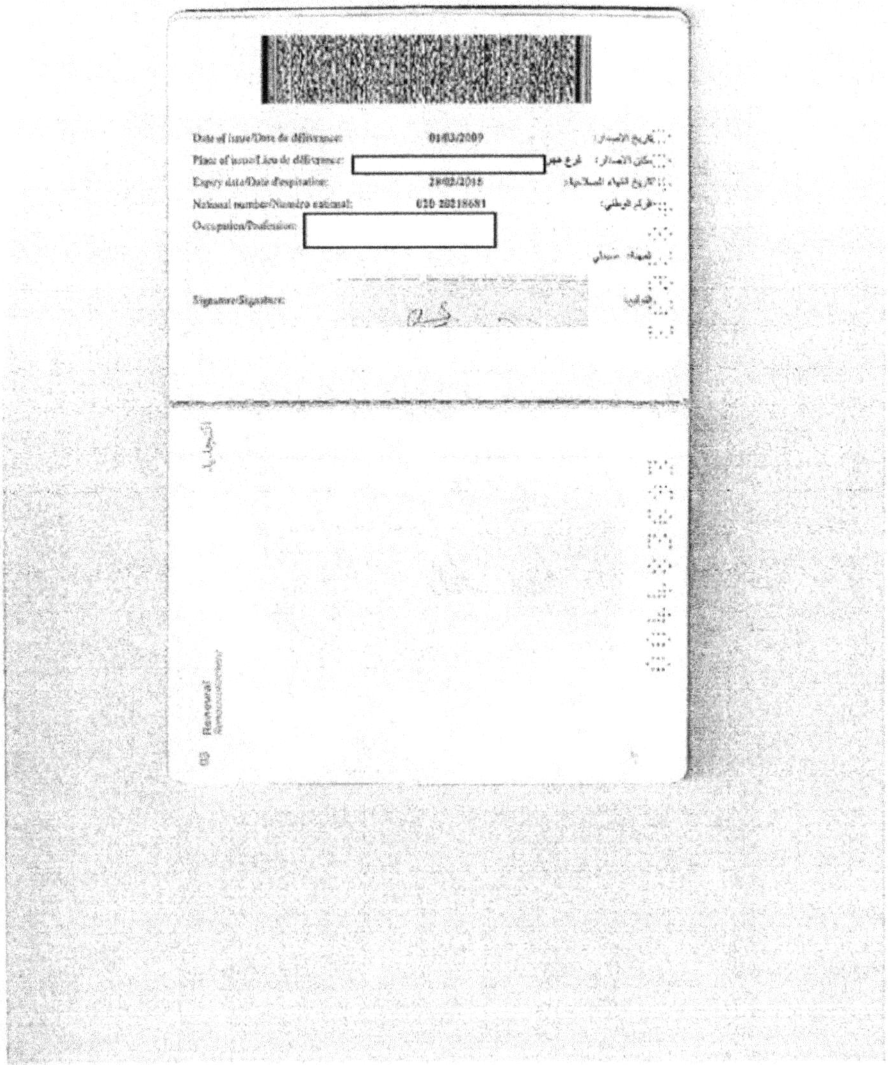

Date of issue/Date de délivrance: 01/03/2009

Place of issue/Lieu de délivrance:

Expiry date/Date d'expiration: 28/02/2015

National number/Numéro national: 020 20218681

Occupation/Profession:

Signature/Signature:

Renewal

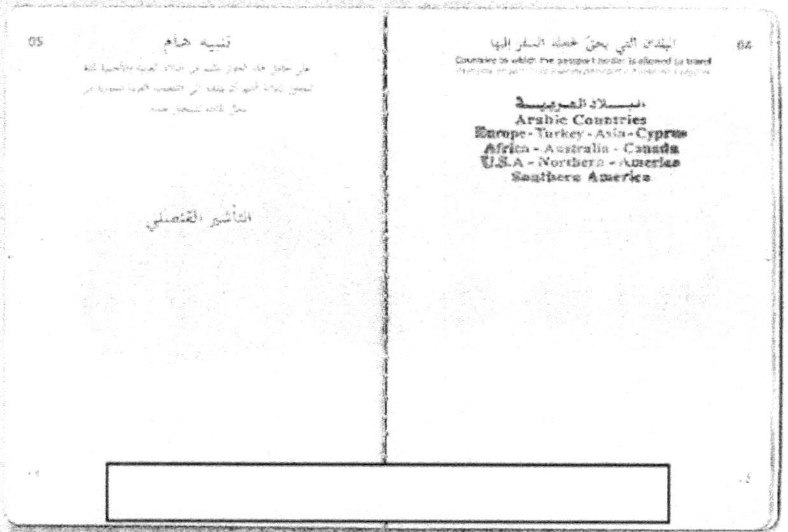

05

تنبيه هام

التأشير القنصلي

04

البلدان التي يحق لحامله السفر إليها

Countries to which the passport holder is allowed to travel

البلاد العربية

Arabic Countries

Europe - Turkey - Asia - Cyprus

Africa - Australia - Canada

U.S.A - Northern - America

Southern America

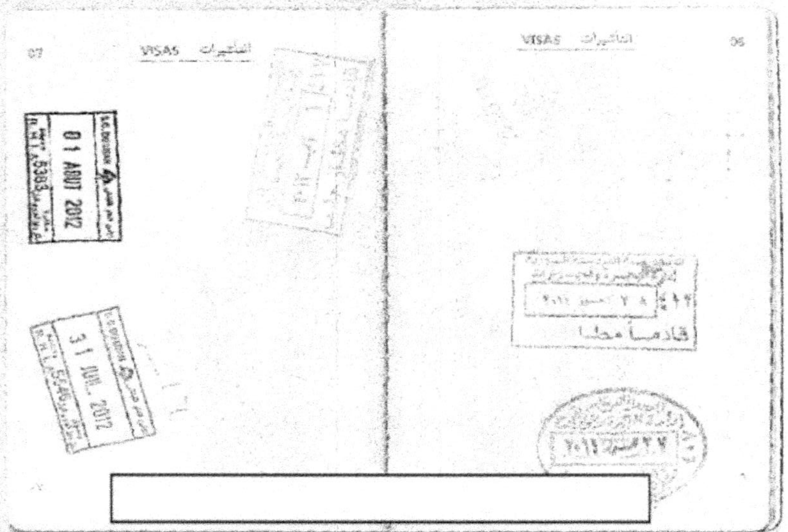
07
VISAS التأشيرات
06
VISAS التأشيرات
S.G.DU LIBAN
01 AOUT 2012
5363
31 JUIL. 2012
5646
قادما محليا

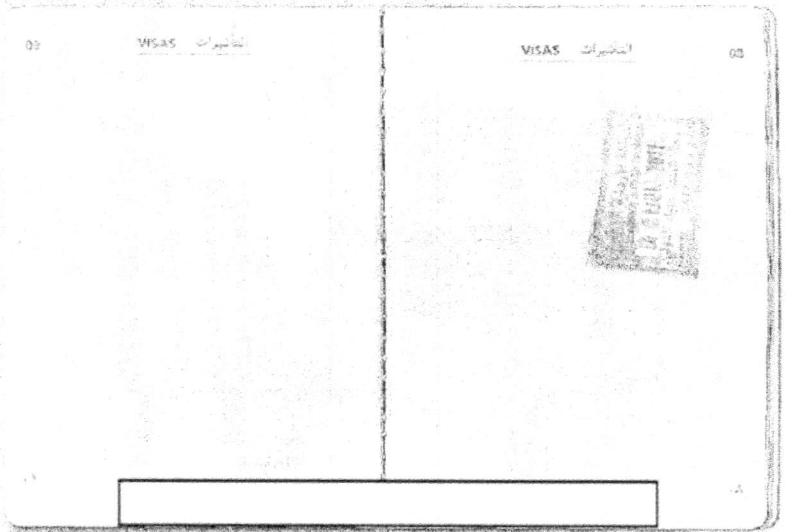
VISAS التأشيرات
VISAS التأشيرات

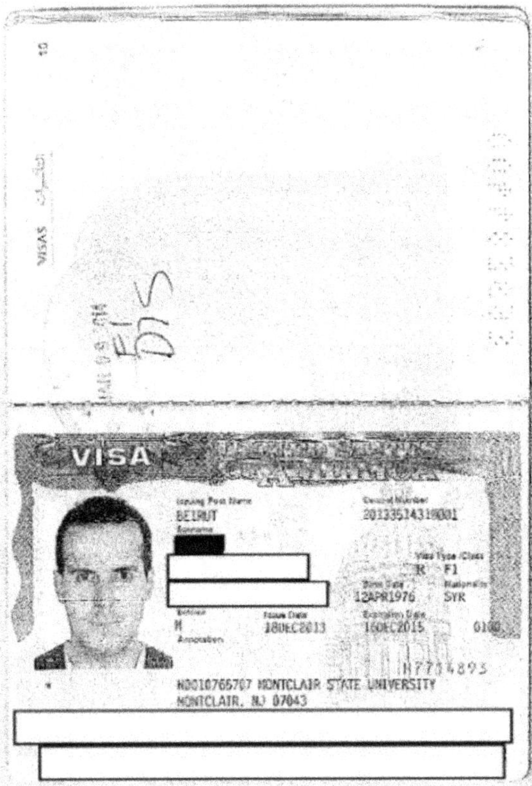
VISAS
VISA
BEIRUT
20133514310001
R F1
12APR1976
SYR
M
18DEC2013
16DEC2015
N0010766707 MONTCLAIR STATE UNIVERSITY
MONTCLAIR, NJ 07043

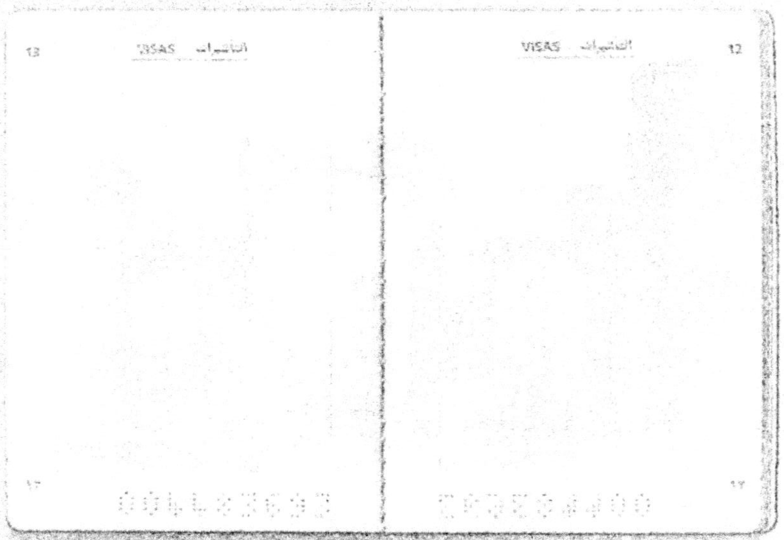
13
VISAS التأشيرات
VISAS التأشيرات
12

15
VISAS التأشيرات
VISAS التأشيرات
14

16
VISAS التأشيرات
17
VISAS التأشيرات

19
VISAS التأشيرات
VISAS التأشيرات
18

21
VISAS
VISAS
20

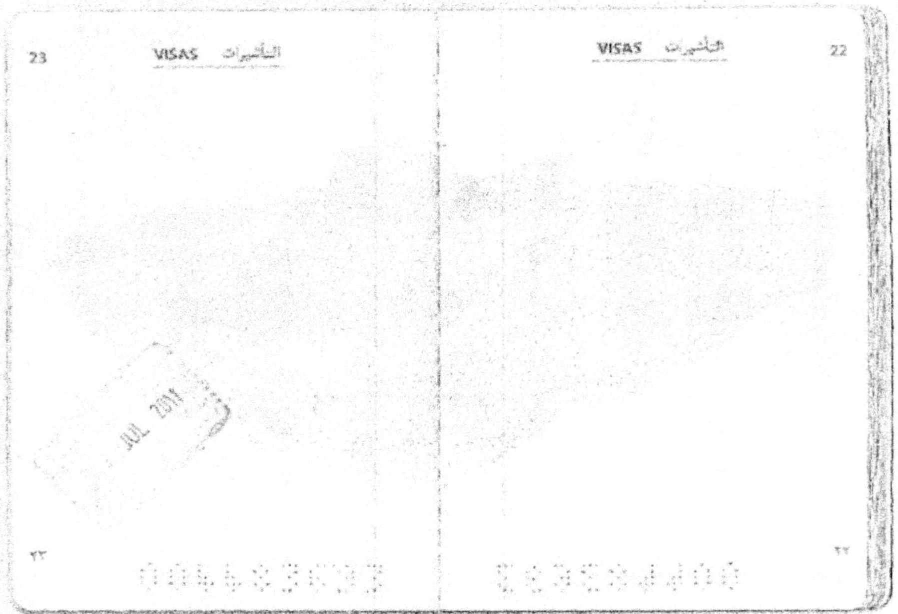
23
VISAS التأشيرات
JUL 2011
VISAS التأشيرات
22

25
VISAS
VISAS
24

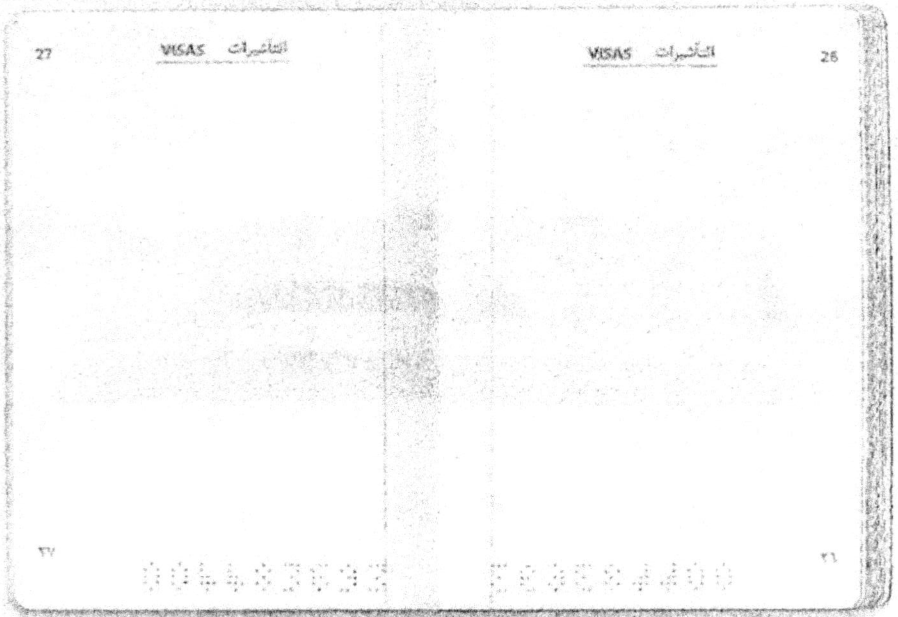
27
VISAS التأشيرات
VISAS التأشيرات
26
٢٧
٢٦

29
VISAS التأشيرات
VISAS التأشيرات
28

31
VISAS التأشيرات
VISAS التأشيرات
30

VISAS تأشيرات
VISAS تأشيرات
32
33

35
VISAS التأشيرات
VISAS التأشيرات
34

37
VISAS التأشيرات
VISAS التأشيرات
36

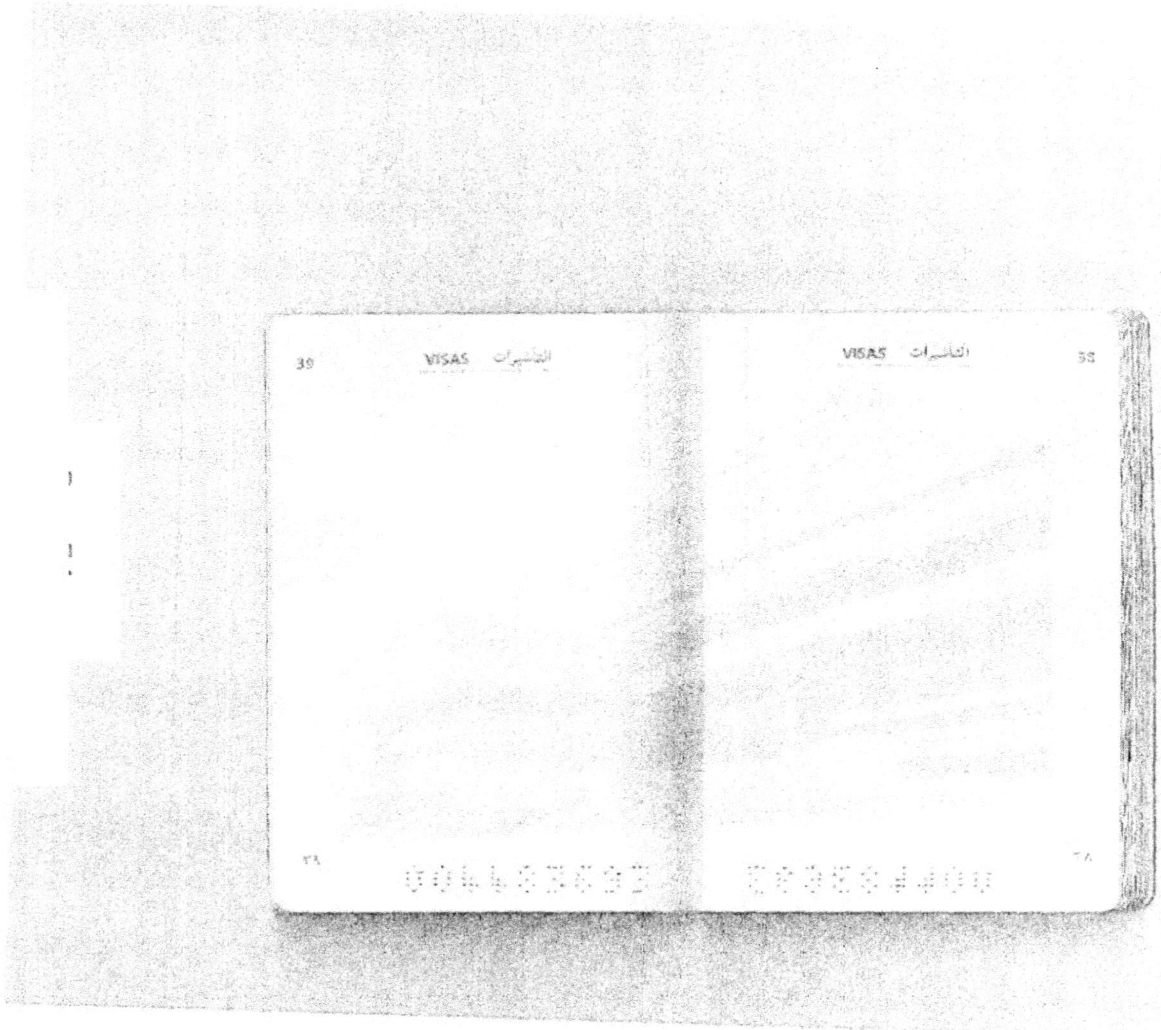
39
VISAS
VISAS

41
VISAS التأشيرات
VISAS التأشيرات
40

43
VISAS التأشيرات
VISAS التأشيرات
42

45
VISAS التأشيرات
VISAS التأشيرات
44

47
VISAS التأشيرات
VISAS التأشيرات
46

VISAS
— SYRIAN PRODUCT —
This passport contains 48 pages

U.S. Customs and Border Protection
Securing America's Borders

OMB No. 1651-0111
Expiration Date: 05/31/2015

Most Recent I-94

Admission (I-94) Record Number: 16650084030

Most Recent Date of Entry: 2014 January 09

Class of Admission: F1

Admit Until Date: D/S

Details provided on the I-94 Information form:

Last/Surname:	[redacted]
First (Given) Name:	
Birth Date:	1976 April 12
Passport Number:	
Country of Issuance:	Syria

Get Travel History

▶ Effective April 26, 2013, DHS began automating the admission process. An alien lawfully admitted or paroled into the U.S. is no longer required to be in possession of a preprinted Form I-94. A record of admission printed from the CBP website constitutes a lawful record of admission. See 8 CFR § 1.4(d).

▶ If an employer, local, state or federal agency requests admission information, present your admission (I-94) number along with any additional required documents requested by that employer or agency.

▶ Note: For security reasons, we recommend that you close your browser after you have finished retrieving your I-94 number.

Exhibit 2: Beneficiary's Bachelor of Pharmacy & Pharmaceutical Chemistry Degree and General Evaluation Report

مكتب راميتا للترجمة RAMITTA TRANSLATION OFFICE	
Ali Muhammad Mehrez Certified Translator in English	علي محمد محرز ترجمان محلف في اللغة الإنكليزية
حلب – خلف الفندق السياحي – سوريا – هاتف : 2120967-2117880	

Syrian Arab Republic
University of Aleppo

No: 052

Certificate
Bachelor of Pharmacy & Pharmaceutical Chemistry
(Industrial Pharmacist)

Pursuant to the decision of Aleppo University Council No.: /1952/ of 18/08/1998

Born in Aleppo in 1976 (nineteen seventy six) of the Syrian Arab Nationality

Has been awarded the degree of:

Bachelor of Pharmacy & Pharmaceutical Chemistry
(Industrial)
With a grade of: Very Good

As a result of the second semester session examinations of the academic year: **1997/1998.**

- Date: 14 September 1998

- Clerk: -- (Signature)
- Verifier: --- (Signature)
- Vice President of Aleppo University: ---------------------------- (Seal & Signature)

- True copy of the original, authenticated by Director of Students Affairs.
  (Seal and Signature)

• True and accurate translation of the Arabic text hereto attached.	
• Aleppo, on 04 November 2012..	• Certified translator: Ali Mehrez

الجمهورية العربية السورية
جامعة حلب

رقم ٠٥٢

مصدقة

الاجازة في الصيدلة والكيمياء الصيدلية

(صيدلي صناعي)

استناداً الى قرار مجلس جامعة حلب رقم ١٩٥٢ تاريخ ١٨ / ٨ / ١٩٩٨

منح السيد عبد المنعم بن محمد صادق قصيد المولود في حلب عام ١٩٧٦

الف وتسعماية وستة وسبعين المتمتع بجنسية عربية سورية

درجة الاجازة في الصيدلة والكيمياء الصيدلية (صناعي) بتقدير جيد جداً .

وذلك بنتيجة امتحانات العام الدراسي ١٩٩٧/١٩٩٨ .

الدورة : الفصلية الثانية

نظم المصدقة　　　دققها

وكيل جامعة حلب

الدكتور محمود كرد

١٤ أيار ١٩٩٨

كل شطب أو حك او تحوير في هذه الوثيقة يلغيها .

لايعطى الطالب سوى مصدقة واحدة واذا احتاج الى اكثر فعليه تصويرها فوتوكوبي وتصديقها من شؤون الطلاب .

ECE®
Educational Credential Evaluators, Inc.
P.O. Box 514070
Milwaukee, Wisconsin 53203-3470 USA
http://www.ece.org
Telephone 414-289-3400

GENERAL EVALUATION REPORT

Name: Reference: 605016/LAM

Date of Birth: 12 April 1976

Purpose: Professional Licensure Date: 5 March 2014

U.S. Equivalence: Bachelor of Pharmacy degree

Credential: Diploma in Pharmacy and Pharmaceutical Chemistry [This is a five-year program that represents the first professional degree in pharmacy in Syria.]

Institution: Aleppo University

Country: Syria

Date: 1998

Comments: The documents submitted indicate graduation at the end of the second semester of the 1997-1998 academic year.
Admission to this program required completion of the United States equivalent of a high school diploma.

Summary

It is the judgment of Educational Credential Evaluators, Inc. that has the United States equivalent of:

~ Bachelor of Pharmacy degree

This evaluation report is based on educational documents submitted according to the requirements of the FPGEC. This evaluation report is a statement of educational equivalence. ECE does not make judgments regarding an individual's eligibility for professional licensure, certification, or registration in the United States.

LAM/rps

605016

Exhibit 3:
Beneficiary's Resume

Applicant Name:

phone :

Harriman lane 2500

Redondo beach

CA , 90278

: Education

: Bachelor in pharmacy and pharmaceutical chemistry-

University of Aleppo /Syria

Graduated 1998

: FPGEC certification-

Issued by National Association of Boards of Pharmacy (NABP) , United States of America . 2014

:certificate in general business: (Management ,marketing ,business administration)-

. University of California Los Angeles , UCLA extension

Expected graduation date : June 2015

: Licenses

.Licensed pharmacist in Syria since 2001-

. Intern pharmacist License in CA : IN PROCESS-

: Experience

. Practitioner pharmacist : 2001-2013 , Aleppo –Syria-

. Pharmacy manager : 2001-2013 , Aleppo –Syria-

: Employment history

. Owner and manager of Retail pharmacy : 2001-2013-

. Languages : English ,Arabic

Exhibit 5: Petitioner's Business Tax Certificate

BUSINESS TAX CERTIFICATE

CITY OF RIALTO

The person, firm or corporation named has paid a business tax in the CITY OF RIALTO, CALIFORNIA, for the business, trade, calling profession, exhibition, or occupation described below, for the period indicated. This license is permission only; not an endorsement of the business activity. The licensee must obtain clearance to conduct business from the Planning and Building Department and agrees to comply with all sections of the Rialto Municipal Code. This business license is NOT TRANSFERABLE.

BUSINESS NAME: INLAND EMPIRE LIVER FOUNDATIO

RATE TYPE DESCRIPTION: EXEMPT

BUSINESS LOCATION: 2006 N RIVERSIDE #A
RIALTO CA 92377

BUSINESS TYPE DESCRIPTION: MEDICAL

BUSINESS OWNER(S) ZEID KAYALI

INLAND EMPIRE LIVER FOUNDATION
2006 N RIVERSIDE #A
RIALTO CA 92377

Business License Number: 1410075

Issue Date: 1/01/2015

Expiration Date: 12/31/2015

Robb R. Steel
Chief Licensing Officer

TO BE POSTED IN A CONSPICUOUS PLACE

NOT TRANSFERABLE

Exhibit 6:
Petitioner's By Laws

BYLAWS
OF
INLAND EMPIRE LIVER FOUNDATION

The name of the organization is Inland Empire Liver Foundation. The organization shall have an office located at 973 S. Los Robles Ave, Pasadena, California, 91106 and at such other places as shall be designated by the board of directors from time to time by resolution. The organization has not been formed for the making of any profit, or personal financial gain. The assets and income of the organization shall not be distributable to, or benefit the trustees, directors, or officers or other individuals. The assets and income shall only be used to promote corporate purposes as described below. Nothing contained herein, however, shall be deemed to prohibit the payment of reasonable compensation to employees and independent contractors for services provided for the benefit of the organization. The organization is organized exclusively for charitable and educational purposes. This organization shall not carry on any other activities not permitted to be carried on by a organization exempt from federal income tax. The organization shall not participate in any political campaign in any manner. The organization shall not attempt to influence legislation. The organization is organized exclusively for charitable, scientific and educational purposes.

ARTICLE I
MEETINGS

Section 1. Annual Meeting. An annual meeting shall be held once each calendar year for the purpose of electing directors and for the transaction of such other business as may properly come before the meeting. The annual meeting shall be held at the time and place designated by the Board of Directors from time to time.

Section 2. Special Meetings. Special meetings maybe be requested by the President or the Board of Directors.

Section 3. Notice. Written notice of all meetings shall be provided under this section or as otherwise required by law. The Notice shall state the place, date, and hour of meeting, and if for a special meeting, the purpose of the meeting. Such notice shall be mailed to all directors of record at the address shown on the corporate books, at least 10 days prior to the meeting. Such notice shall be deemed effective when deposited in ordinary U.S. mail, properly addressed, with postage prepaid.

Section 4. Place of Meeting. Meetings shall be held at the corporation's principal place of business unless otherwise stated in the notice.

Section 5. Quorum. A majority of the directors shall constitute at quorum at a meeting. In the absence of a quorum, a majority of the directors may adjourn the meeting to another time without further notice. If a quorum is represented at an adjourned meeting, any business may be transacted that might have been transacted at the meeting as originally scheduled. The directors present at a meeting represented by a quorum may continue to transact business until adjournment, even if the withdrawal of some directors results in representation of less than a quorum.

Section 6. Informal Action. Any action required to be taken, or which may be taken, at a meeting, may be taken without a meeting and without prior notice if a consent in writing, setting forth the action so taken, is signed by the directors with respect to the subject matter of the vote.

ARTICLE II
DIRECTORS

Section 1. Number of Directors. The corporation shall be managed by a Board of Directors consisting of 5 director(s).

Section 2. Election and Term of Office. The directors shall be elected at the annual meeting. Each director shall serve a term of 3 years year(s), or until a successor has been elected and qualified.

Section 3. Quorum. A majority of directors shall constitute a quorum.

Section 4. Adverse Interest. In the determination of a quorum of the directors, or in voting, the adverse interest of a director shall not disqualify the director or invalidate his or her vote.

Section 5. Organizational Meeting of Board. The Board of Directors shall meet immediately after the election for the purpose of electing its new officers, appointing new committee chairpersons and for transacting such other business as may be deemed appropriate.

Section 6. Regular Meeting. The Board of Directors shall have regular meetings every quarter, the schedule of which shall be established at the annual meeting, to accomplish the business of the organization. No notice of such meetings shall be required.

Section 7. Special Meeting. Special meetings may be requested by the President, Vice-President, Secretary, or any two directors by providing five days' written notice by ordinary United States mail, effective when mailed. Minutes of the meeting shall be sent to the Board of Directors within two weeks after the meeting.

Section 8. Procedures. The vote of a majority of the directors present at a properly called meeting at which a quorum is present shall be the act of the Board of Directors, unless the vote of a greater number is required by law or by these by-laws for a particular resolution. A director of the organization who is present at a meeting of the Board of Directors at which action on any corporate matter is taken shall be presumed to have assented to the action taken unless their dissent shall be entered in the minutes of the meeting. The Board shall keep written minutes of its proceedings in its permanent records.

Section 9. Emergency Action. Should action be required when it is not possible to assemble the Board of Directors in a properly called meeting or when the Executive committee explicitly cannot assume the powers of the full board, written or oral approval of the proposed action by a board majority may beobtained in a poll of the entire Board of Directors authorized by the President or majority of the Executive committee. Any action so taken shall be recorded in the minutes of the next properly called board meeting.

Section 10. **Informal Action.** Any action required to be taken at a meeting of directors, or any action which may be taken at a meeting of directors or of a committee of directors, may be taken without a meeting if a consent in writing setting forth the action so taken, is signed by all of the directors or all of the members of the committee of directors, as the case may be.

Section 11. **Removal / Vacancies.** A director shall be subject to removal, with or without cause, at a meeting called for that purpose. Any vacancy that occurs on the Board of Directors, whether by death, resignation, removal or any other cause, may be filled by the remaining directors. A director elected to fill a vacancy shall serve the remaining term of his or her predecessor, or until a successor has been elected and qualified.

Section 12. **Standing Committees.** There shall be three (3) standing committees of the organization: executive, nominating and fund-raising/public relations. The President shall appoint the chairpersons of all committees from the membership of the Board of Directors of the organization with the approval of the Board of Directors. All committee appointments shall terminate upon the election of a new President, unless specifically determined otherwise at the Annual meeting. All committees shall function within the guidelines and budgets established by the Board of Directors.

Section 13. **Executive Committee.** The Executive Committee shall be composed of the officers of the organization, as specified herein, and shall have the full authority to undertake the duties and powers of the board except as these by-laws specifically state otherwise. All actions of the Executive Committee shall be reported to the board at its next meeting.

Section 14. **Ad Hoc Committees.** The President may establish ad hoc committees at any time. All ad hoc committees are subject to the same rules and operating procedures as standing committees.

Section 15. **Budgets.** The Board of Directors shall approve the annual budget of the organization during the first quarter of each calendar year upon recommendation of the Executive Committee.

Section 16. **Personnel Responsibilities.** The Board of Directors may employ and discharge employees of the organization and may prescribe their duties and compensation. The board shall discharge its duties with respect to personnel organizational matters without regard to age, sex, race, color, creed, sexual orientation, or the national origin of any person.

Section 17. **Records.** Every Director shall have the absolute right at any reasonable time to inspect and copy all books, records and documents of every kind and to inspect the physical properties of the organization.

Section 18. **Compensation.** No board member or officer of or any member of a committee shall receive at any time any of the net earnings or profit from the operations of the organization. However, this shall not prevent the payment to any such person of reasonable compensation for services rendered to or for the organization. Such compensation shall be fixed by the Board of Directors from time to time.

ARTICLE III
OFFICERS

Section 1. Number of Officers. The officers of the corporation shall be a President, one or more Vice-Presidents (as determined by the Board of Directors), a Secretary, and a Treasurer. Two or more offices may be held by one person.

a. President. The President shall be the chief executive officer and shall preside at all meetings of the Board of Directors and its Executive Committee.

b. Vice President. The Vice President shall perform the duties of the President in the absence of the President and shall assist that office in the discharge of its leadership duties.

c. Secretary. The Secretary shall give notice of all meetings of the Board of Directors and Executive Committee, shall keep an accurate list of the directors, and shall have the authority to certify any records, or copies of records, as the official records of the organization. The Secretary shall maintain the minutes of the Board of Directors' meetings and all committee meetings.

d. Treasurer. The Treasurer shall be responsible for conducting the financial affairs of the organization as directed and authorized by the Board of Directors and Executive Committee, and shall make reports of corporate finances as required, but no less often than at each meeting of the Board of Directors and Executive Committee.

Section 2. Term of Office. The officers shall be elected annually by the Board of Directors at the first meeting of the Board of Directors. Each officer shall serve a one year term or until a successor has been elected and qualified.

Section 3. Elections. The nominating committee, a standing committee of the organization, shall nominate, at least thirty (30) days prior to the annual meeting, a slate of qualified candidates for the director position whose terms are to expire or are vacant, and its slate of candidates shall be included with the notice of the annual meeting. Following the report of the nominating committee at the meeting, any director of the organization may nominate other candidates for the available director positions, provided that the nominees agree to serve if elected. At the conclusion of nominations, the Board of Directors shall vote for each position by secret written ballot.

Section 4. Removal or Vacancy. The Board of Directors shall have the power to remove an officer or agent of the corporation. Any vacancy that occurs for any reason may be filled by the Board of Directors.

ARTICLE IV
CORPORATE SEAL, EXECUTION OF INSTRUMENTS

The corporation shall not have a corporate seal. All instruments that are executed on behalf of the corporation which are acknowledged and which affect an interest in real estate shall be executed by the President or any Vice-President and the Secretary or Treasurer. All other instruments executed by the corporation, including a release of mortgage or lien, may be executed by the President or any Vice-President. Notwithstanding the preceding provisions of this section, any written instrument may be executed by any officer(s) or agent(s) that are specifically designated by resolution of the Board of Directors.

ARTICLE V
AMENDMENT TO BYLAWS

The bylaws may be amended, altered, or repealed by the Board of Directors by a majority of a quorum vote at any regular or special meeting. The text of the proposed change shall be distributed to all board members at least ten (10) days before the meeting.

ARTICLE VI
INDEMNIFICATION

Any director or officer who is involved in litigation by reason of his or her position as a director or officer of this corporation shall be indemnified and held harmless by the corporation to the fullest extent authorized by law as it now exists or may subsequently be amended (but, in the case of any such amendment, only to the extent that such amendment permits the corporation to provide broader indemnification rights).

ARTICLE VII
DISSOLUTION

In the event of the dissolution of the organization, the assets shall be applied and distributed as follows:

All liabilities and obligations shall be paid, satisfied and discharged, or adequate provision shall be made therefor. Assets not held upon a condition requiring return, transfer, or conveyance to any other organization or individual shall be distributed, transferred, or conveyed, in trust or otherwise, to charitable and educational organization, organized under Section 501(c)(3) of the Internal Revenue Code of 1986, as amended, of a similar or like nature to this organization, as determined by the Board of Directors.

Exhibit 8:
Online Wage Library

Online Wage Library - FLC Wage Search Results

Tuesday, March 31, 2015 New Quick Search New Search Wizard

You selected the All Industries database for 7/2014 - 6/2015. Your search returned the following:

Area Code:	40140
Area Title:	Riverside-San Bernardino-Ontario, CA MSA
GeoLevel:	1
OES/SOC Code:	19-2031
OES/SOC Title:	Chemists
Level 1 Wage:	\$18.60 hour - \$38,688 year
Level 2 Wage:	\$24.78 hour - \$51,542 year
Level 3 Wage:	\$30.95 hour - \$64,376 year
Level 4 Wage:	\$37.13 hour - \$77,230 year
Mean Wage (H-2B):	\$30.95 hour - \$64,376 year

This wage applies to the following O*Net occupations:
19-2031.00 Chemists

Conduct qualitative and quantitative chemical analyses or experiments in laboratories for quality or process control or to develop new products or knowledge.
O*Net™ JobZone: 4 -- Education & Training Code: 5-Bachelor's degree

The prevailing wage must be at, or above the federal or state or local minimum wage, whichever is higher. The federal minimum wage is \$7.25/hr effective July 24, 2009.

Exhibit 9: Occupational Outlook Handbook

U.S. Bureau of Labor Statistics

Chemists and Materials Scientists

Summary

Chemists and materials scientists perform experiments that require creative problem solving and detailed record keeping.

Quick Facts: Chemists and Materials Scientists	
2012 Median Pay	$73,060 per year $35.13 per hour
Entry-Level Education	Bachelor's degree
Work Experience in a Related Occupation	None
On-the-job Training	None
Number of Jobs, 2012	96,200
Job Outlook, 2012-22	6% (Slower than average)
Employment Change, 2012-22	5,400

What Chemists and Materials Scientists Do

Chemists and materials scientists study substances at the atomic and molecular levels and the ways in which substances react with each other. They use their knowledge to develop new and improved products and to test the quality of manufactured goods.

Work Environment

Chemists and materials scientists work in laboratories and offices. They typically work full time and keep regular hours.

How to Become a Chemist or Materials Scientist

Chemists and materials scientists need at least a bachelor's degree in chemistry or a related field. However, a master's degree or Ph.D. is needed for many research jobs.

Pay

In May 2012, the median annual wage for chemis [illegible] nnual wage of materials scientists was $88,990 in May 2012.

Job Outlook

Employment of chemists and materials scientists is projected to grow 6 percent from 2012 to 2022, slower than the average for all occupations. Chemists and materials scientists with an advanced degree, particularly those with a Ph.D., are expected to experience better opportunities.

Similar Occupations

Compare the job duties, education, job growth, and pay of chemists and materials scientists with similar occupations.

More Information, Including Links to O*NET

Learn more about chemists and materials scientists by visiting additional resources, including O*NET, a source on key characteristics of workers and occupations.

What Chemists and Materials Scientists Do

Most chemists and materials scientists work as part of a team.

Chemists and materials scientists study substances at the atomic and molecular levels and the ways in which substances react with each other. They use their knowledge to develop new and improved products and to test the quality of manufactured goods.

Duties

Chemists and materials scientists typically do the following:

- Plan and carry out complex research projects, such as the development of new products and testing methods
- Direct technicians and other workers in testing and analyzing components and the physical properties of materials
- Instruct scientists and technicians on proper chemical processing and testing procedures, such as ingredients, mixing times, and operating temperatures
- Prepare solutions, compounds, and reagents used in laboratory procedures
- Analyze substances to determine their composition and concentration of elements
- Conduct tests on materials and other substances, to ensure that safety and quality standards are met
- Write technical reports that detail methods and findings
- Present research findings to scientists, engineers, and other colleagues

Many chemists and materials scientists work in basic and applied research. In basic research, chemists investigate the properties, composition, and structure of matter. They also experiment with combinations of elements and the ways in which they interact. In applied research, chemists investigate possible new products and ways to improve existing ones. Chemistry research has led to the discovery and [illegible] oved drugs, plastics, cleaners, and thousands of other products.

Materials scientists study the structures and chemical properties of various materials, to develop new products or enhance existing ones. They determine ways to strengthen or combine materials or develop new materials for use in a variety of products. Applications of materials science include inventing or improving superconducting materials, ceramics, and metallic alloys.

Chemists and materials scientists use computers and a wide variety of sophisticated laboratory instrumentation for modeling, simulation, and experimental analysis. For example, some chemists use three-dimensional (3D) computer modeling software to study the structure and other properties of complex molecules.

Most chemists and materials scientists work as part of a team. An increasing number of scientific research projects involve multiple disciplines, and it is common for chemists and materials scientists to work on teams with other scientists, such as biologists and physicists, computer specialists, and engineers. For example, in pharmaceutical research, chemists may work with biologists to develop new drugs and with engineers to design ways to mass produce the new drugs. For more information, see the profiles on biochemists and biophysicists, microbiologists, zoologists and wildlife biologists, physicists and astronomers, computer and information technology occupations, and engineers.

Chemists often specialize in a particular branch of the field. The following are examples of some types of chemists:

Analytical chemists determine the structure, composition, and nature of substances, by examining and identifying their various elements or compounds. They also study the relationships and interactions between the parts of compounds. Some analytical chemists specialize in developing new methods of analysis and new techniques for carrying out their work. Their research has a wide range of applications, including food safety, pharmaceuticals, and pollution control.

Inorganic chemists study the structure, properties, and reactions of molecules that do not contain carbon, such as metals. They work to understand the behavior and the characteristics of inorganic substances. Inorganic chemists figure out how these materials can be modified, separated, or used in products, such as ceramics and superconductors.

Medicinal chemists research and develop chemical compounds that can be used as pharmaceutical drugs. They work on teams with other scientists and engineers to create and test new drug products. They also help develop new and improved manufacturing processes to produce new drugs on a large scale effectively.

Organic chemists study the structure, properties, and reactions of molecules that contain carbon. They also design and make new organic substances that have unique properties and applications. These compounds have, in turn, been used to develop many commercial products, such as pharmaceutical drugs and plastics.

Physical chemists study the fundamental characteristics of how matter behaves on a molecular and atomic level and how chemical reactions occur. Based on their analyses, physical chemists may develop new theories, such as how complex structures are formed. Physical chemists often work closely with materials scientists, to research and develop potential uses for new materials.

Theoretical chemists investigate theoretical methods that can predict the outcomes of chemical experiments. Theoretical chemistry encompasses a variety of specializations itself, though most specializations incorporate advanced computation and programming. Some examples of theoretical chemists are computational chemists, mathematical chemists, and chemical informaticians.

Materials scientists tend to specialize by the material they work with most often. A few examples of materials in which these scientists specialize are ceramics, glass, semiconductors, and composite materials.

A growing numbers of chemists work in interdisciplinary fields, such as biochemistry and geochemistry. For more information, see the profile on geoscientists.

Many people with a chemistry background become professors or teachers. For more information, see the profiles on high school teachers and postsecondary teachers.

Work Environment

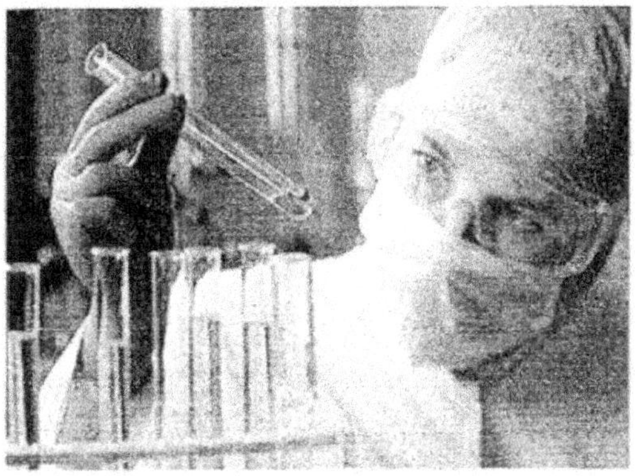

Chemists must wear protective clothing such as gloves and goggles when handling hazardous chemicals.

Chemists and material scientists held about 96,200 jobs in 2012. The industries that employed the most chemists in 2012 were as follows:

Research and development in the physical, engineering, and life sciences	20%
Pharmaceutical and medicine manufacturing	17
Testing laboratories	11
Federal government, excluding postal service	7
State and local government, excluding education and hospitals	6

Most materials scientists work in manufacturing and scientific research and development. The industries that employed the most materials scientists in 2012 were as follows:

Research and development in the physical, engineering, and life sciences	34%
Colleges, universities, and professional schools; state, local, and private	11
Pharmaceutical and medicine manufacturing	6
Computer and electronic product manufacturing	6
Basic chemical manufacturing	5

Chemists and materials scientists typically work in laboratories and offices, where they conduct experiments and analyze their results. In addition to laboratories, materials scientists work with engineers and processing specialists in industrial manufacturing facilities. Some chemists also work in these facilities and usually are responsible for monitoring the environmental conditions at the plant. Chemists and materials scientists, who work for manufacturing companies, may have to travel occasionally, especially if their company has multiple facilities.

Chemists and materials scientists typically work on research teams. They need to be able to work well with others towards a common goal. Many serve in a leadership capacity and need to be able to motivate and direct other team members.

Injuries and Illnesses

Chemists and materials scientists can be exposed to health or safety hazards when handling certain chemicals, but there is little risk if proper procedures are followed.

Work Schedules

(ally work rs.

How to Become a Chemist or Materials Scientist

Most chemists and materials scientists work in laboratories.

Chemists and materials scientists need at least a bachelor's degree in chemistry or a related field. However, a master's degree or Ph.D. is needed for many research jobs.

Education

A bachelor's degree in chemistry or in a related field is needed for entry-level chemist jobs. Although some materials scientists hold a degree in materials science, these scientists commonly have a degree in chemistry, physics, or engineering. Many jobs require master's degrees or Ph.D.s and may also require significant levels of work experience. Chemists and materials scientists with Ph.D.s and postdoctoral experience typically lead basic and applied research teams.

Many colleges and universities offer degree programs in chemistry. There are few programs specifically in materials science, but the number of programs is gradually increasing. Some engineering schools offer degrees in the joint field of materials science and engineering.

Undergraduate chemistry majors typically are required to take courses in analytical, organic, inorganic, and physical chemistry. In addition to chemistry coursework, they also take classes in mathematics, biological sciences, and physics. Computer science courses are essential, because chemists and materials scientists need computer skills to perform modeling and simulation tasks, manage and manipulate databases, and to operate computerized laboratory equipment.

Laboratory experience, either at a college or university, or through internships, fellowships, or work-study programs in industry, is also useful.

Graduate students studying chemistry commonly specialize in a subfield, such as analytical chemistry or inorganic chemistry. For example, those interested in doing research in the pharmaceutical industry usually develop a strong background in medicinal or organic chemistry.

Important Qualities

Analytical skills. Chemists and materials scientists carry out scientific experiments and studies. They must be precise and accurate in their analyses, because errors could invalidate their research.

Communication skills. Chemists and materials scientists need to communicate with team members and other scientists. They must be able to read and write technical reports and give presentations.

Critical-thinking skills. Chemists and materials scientists carefully evaluate their own work and the work of others. They must determine if results and conclusions are based on sound science.

Mathematical skills. Chemists and materials scientists regularly use complex mathematical equations and formulas, and they need a broad understanding of mathematics, and statistics.

Organizational skills. Chemists and materials scientists need to carefully document processes to conform to regulations and industry procedures. Disorganization in the workplace can lead to legal problems, damage to equipment, and chemical spills.

Problem-solving skills. Chemists and materials scientists research and develop new and improved chemical products, processes, and materials. This work requires a great deal of trial and error on the part of chemists and materials scientists before a unique solution is found.

Advancement

Chemists typically receive greater responsibility and independence in their work as they gain experience. Greater responsibility also is gained through further education. Ph.D. chemists usually lead research teams and have control over the direction and content of projects, but even Ph.D. holders have room to advance as they gain experience. They may take on larger, more complicated, and more expensive projects as they become more proficient in managing research projects.

Some chemists and materials scientists become natural sciences managers.

Pay

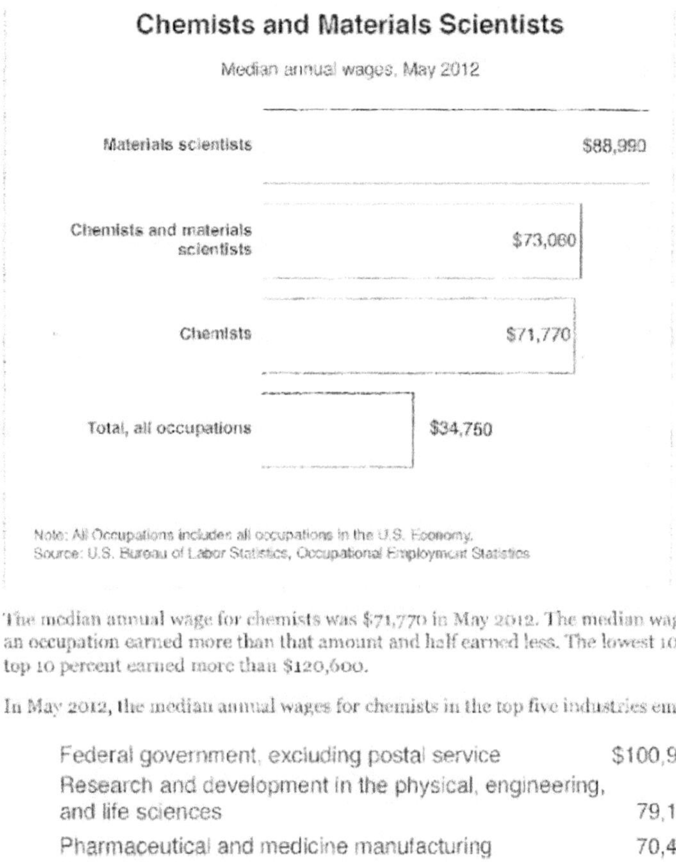

The median annual wage for chemists was $71,770 in May 2012. The median wage is the wage at which half the workers in an occupation earned more than that amount and half earned less. The lowest 10 percent earned less than $41,080, and the top 10 percent earned more than $120,600.

In May 2012, the median annual wages for chemists in the top five industries employing these scientists were as follows:

Federal government, excluding postal service	$100,920
Research and development in the physical, engineering, and life sciences	79,140
Pharmaceutical and medicine manufacturing	70,480
State and local government, excluding education and hospitals	57,190
Testing laboratories	[illegible],060

The median annual wage for materials scientists was $88,990 in May 2012. The lowest 10 percent earned less than $46,960, and the top 10 percent earned more than $134,130.

In May 2012, the median annual wages for materials scientists in the top five industries employing these scientists were as follows:

Basic chemical manufacturing	$106,770
Research and development in the physical, engineering, and life sciences	96,630
Computer and electronic product manufacturing	96,620
Colleges, universities, and professional schools; state, local, and private	66,720
Pharmaceutical and medicine manufacturing	66,230

Chemists and materials scientists typically work full time and keep regular hours.

Job Outlook

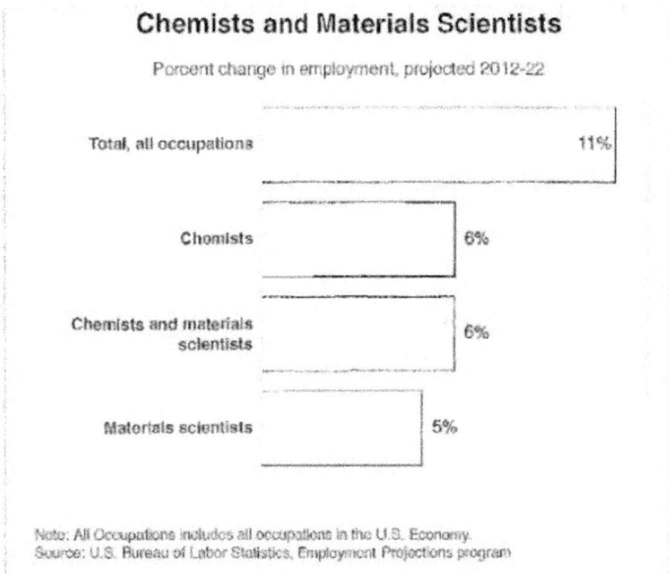

Employment of chemists and materials scientists is projected to grow 6 percent from 2012 to 2022, slower than the average for all occupations.

Employment of chemists is projected to grow 6 percent, as they will continue to be needed in scientific research and development and to monitor the quality of products and processes.

Employment of materials scientists is projected to grow 5 percent, owing to demand for cheaper, safer, and better quality materials for a variety of purposes, such as electronics, energy, and transportation.

Chemists research and solve a wide range of problems and are employed in a similarly wide range of industries. About a quarter of all chemists are employed in chemical manufacturing industries; but the remainder work at colleges and universities, in government, and for independent testing and research laboratories. Some chemical manufacturing industries, such as pharmaceutical manufacturing, increasingly may be outsourcing their research and development activities, rather than doing the research in-hous[illegible] r growth in the employment of chemists in small, independent research and development fir[illegible] nal large manufacturers. However, as the economy improves and the expansion in domesti[illegible] rs the cost of energy and raw inputs, manufacturers may have less of an incentive than they have in the past to outsource their research and development (R&D) activities.

Environmental research will offer many new opportunities for chemists and materials scientists. For example, chemical manufacturing industries will continue to develop technologies and processes that reduce pollution and improve energy efficiency at manufacturing facilities. Chemists also will continue to be needed to monitor pollution levels at manufacturing facilities and to ensure compliance with local, state, and federal environmental regulations.

Job Prospects

In addition to job openings resulting from employment growth, some job openings will result from the need to replace chemists and materials scientists who retire or otherwise leave the occupations.

Chemists and materials scientists with advanced degrees, particularly those with a Ph.D. and work experience, are expected to experience better opportunities. Large pharmaceutical and biotechnology firms provide openings for these workers at research laboratories, and many others work in colleges and universities. Furthermore, chemists with advanced degrees will continue to fill most senior research and upper-management positions.

Employment projections data for Chemists and Materials Scientists, 2012-22

Occupational Title	SOC Code	Employment, 2012	Projected Employment, 2022	Change, 2012-22		Employment by Industry
				Percent	Numeric	
Chemists and materials scientists	—	96,200	101,600	6	5,400	—
Chemists	19-2031	87,900	92,900	6	5,000	[XLS]
Materials scientists	19-2032	8,300	8,800	5	400	[XLS]

SOURCE: U.S. Bureau of Labor Statistics, Employment Projections program

Similar Occupations

This table shows a list of occupations with job duties that are similar to those of chemists and materials scientists.

	OCCUPATION	JOB DUTIES	ENTRY-LEVEL EDUCATION	2012 MEDIAN PAY
	Agricultural and Food Scientists	Agricultural and food scientists work to ensure that agricultural establishments are productive and food is safe.	See How to Become One	$58,610
	Biochemists and Biophysicists	Biochemists and biophysicists study the chemical and physical principles of living things and of biological processes, such as cell development, growth, and heredity.	Doctoral or professional degree	$81,480
		Chemical engineers apply the principles of chemistry, biology, physics, and math to solve problems that involve the production or use fuel, drugs, food, a other products. Th		

	Engineers	processes and equipment for large-scale safe and sustainable manufacturing, plan and test methods of manufacturing products and treating byproducts, and supervise production.	Bachelor's degree	$94,350
	Environmental Scientists and Specialists	Environmental scientists and specialists use their knowledge of the natural sciences to protect the environment and human health. They may clean up polluted areas, advise policy makers, or work with industry to reduce waste.	Bachelor's degree	$63,570
	Geoscientists	Geoscientists study the physical aspects of the Earth, such as its composition, structure, and processes, to learn about its past, present, and future.	Bachelor's degree	$90,890
	High School Teachers	High school teachers help prepare students for life after graduation. They teach academic lessons and various skills that students will need to attend college and to enter the job market.	Bachelor's degree	$55,050
	Materials Engineers	Materials engineers develop, process, and test materials used to create a range of products, from computer chips and aircraft wings to golf clubs and snow skis. They work with metals, ceramics, plastics, composites, and other substances to create new materials that meet certain mechanical, electrical, and chemical requirements.	Bachelor's degree	$85,150
	Natural Sciences Managers	Natural sciences managers supervise the work of scientists, including chemists, physicists, and biologists. They direct activities related to research and development, and coordinate activities such as testing, quality control, and production.	Bachelor's degree	$115,730
		Physicists and astronomers study the ways in which various forms of matter and energy interact. Th physicists and astr		

	**Physicists and Astronomers**	may study the nature of time or the origin of the universe. Physicists and astronomers in applied fields may develop new military technologies or new sources of energy, or monitor space debris that could endanger satellites.	Doctoral or professional degree	$106,360
	**Postsecondary Teachers**	Postsecondary teachers instruct students in a wide variety of academic and vocational subjects beyond the high school level. They also conduct research and publish scholarly papers and books.	See How to Become One	$68,970

Contacts for More Information

For information on career opportunities, earnings, and education for chemists and materials scientists, visit

American Chemical Society

American Chemistry Council

ASM International

Materials Research Society

To find job openings for chemists in the federal government, visit

USAJOBS

O*NET

Materials Scientists

Chemists

Suggested citation:

Bureau of Labor Statistics, U.S. Department of Labor, *Occupational Outlook Handbook, 2014-15 Edition*, Chemists and Materials Scientists, on the Internet at http://www.bls.gov/ooh/life-physical-and-social-science/chemists-and-materials-scientists.htm (visited *March 31, 2015*).

Publish Date: Wednesday, January 8, 2014

Exhibit 10: O*Net Online Summary

O*NET OnLine

Updated 2013

green

Summary Report for:

19-2031.00 - Chemists

Conduct qualitative and quantitative chemical analyses or experiments in laboratories for quality or process control or to develop new products or knowledge.

Sample of reported job titles: Air Quality Chemist, Analytical Chemist, Chemical Laboratory Scientist, Chemist, Forensic Chemist, Forensic Scientist, Quality Control Chemist (QC Chemist), Research Chemist, Scientist, Senior Chemist

View report: Summary | Details | Custom

Tasks | Tools & Technology | Knowledge | Skills | Abilities | Work Activities | Work Context | Job Zone | Education | Credentials | Interests | Work Styles | Work Values | Related Occupations | Wages & Employment | Job Openings | Additional Information

Tasks

- Analyze organic or inorganic compounds to determine chemical or physical properties, composition, structure, relationships, or reactions, using chromatography, spectroscopy, or spectrophotometry techniques.
- Conduct quality control tests.
- Maintain laboratory instruments to ensure proper working order and troubleshoot malfunctions when needed.
- Prepare test solutions, compounds, or reagents for laboratory personnel to conduct tests.
- Induce changes in composition of substances by introducing heat, light, energy, or chemical catalysts for quantitative or qualitative analysis.
- Evaluate laboratory safety procedures to ensure compliance with standards or to make improvements as needed.
- Compile and analyze test information to determine process or equipment operating efficiency or to diagnose malfunctions.
- Write technical papers or reports or prepare standards and specifications for processes, facilities, products, or tests.
- Confer with scientists or engineers to conduct analyses of research projects, interpret test results, or develop nonstandard tests.
- Develop, improve, or customize products, equipment, formulas, processes, or analytical methods.

back to top

Tools & Technology

Tools used in this occupation:

Benchtop centrifuges — Chemical centrifuges; High-speed centrifuges; Tabletop centrifuges

Calorimeters — Differential scanning calorimeters; Oxygen bomb calorimeters

Lasers — Diode lasers; Helium-cadmium lasers; Nitrogen lasers; Picosecond lasers

Spectrometers — Luminescence spectrometers; Ultraviolet-visible spectrometers

Titration equipment — Autotitrators; Karl Fischer titrators; Titrators

Technology used in this occupation:

Analytical or scientific software — Agilent ChemStation; Bruker BioSpin TopSpin; Waters Empower Chromatography Data Software; Wavefunction Spartan

Computer aided design CAD software — ChemInnovation Software Chem 4-D; ChemSW Molecular Modeling Pro; Hypercube HyperChem

Data base user interface and query software — ChemSW Buffer Maker; JDA Arthur KnowledgeBase database; LabTrack Electronic Lab Notebook; Molsearch Pro

Graphics or photo imaging software — Digital imaging software; Graphics software; MolDraw *

Office suite software — Apple iWork software; Microsoft Office software; NeoOffice *

* Software developed by a government agency and/or distributed as freeware or shareware.

back to top

Knowledge

Chemistry — Knowledge of the chemical composition, structure, and properties of substances and of the chemical processes and transformations that they undergo. This includes uses of chemicals and their interactions, danger signs, production techniques, and disposal methods.

Mathematics — Knowledge of arithmetic, algebra, geometry, calculus, statistics, and their applications.

Production and Processing — Knowledge of raw materials, production processes, quality control, costs, and other techniques for maximizing the effective manufacture and distribution of goods.

Computers and Electronics — Knowledge of circuit boards, processors, chips, electronic equipment, and computer hardware and software, including applications and programming.

English Language — Knowledge of the structure and content of the English language including the meaning and spelling of words, rules of composition, and grammar.

Customer and Personal Service — Knowledge of principles and processes for providing customer and personal services. This includes customer needs assessment, meeting quality standards for services, and evaluation of customer satisfaction.

Engineering and Technology — Knowledge of the practical application of engineering science and technology. This includes applying principles, techniques, procedures, and equipment to the design and production of various goods and services.

back to top

Skills

Science — Using scientific rules and methods to solve problems.

Critical Thinking — Using logic and reasoning to identify the strengths and weaknesses of alternative solutions, conclusions or approaches to problems.

Reading Comprehension — Understanding written sentences and paragraphs in work related documents.

Active Listening — Giving full attention to what other people are saying, taking time to understand the points being made, asking questions as appropriate, and not interrupting at inappropriate times.

Mathematics — Using mathematics to solve problems.

Complex Problem Solving — Identifying complex problems and reviewing related information to develop and evaluate options and implement solutions.

Writing — Communicating effectively in writing as appropriate for the needs of the audience.

Speaking — Talking to others to convey information effectively.

Active Learning — Understanding the implicati [illegible] oth current and future problem-solving and decision-making.

Quality Control Analysis — Conducting tests and inspections of products, services, or processes to evaluate quality or performance.

back to top

Abilities

Deductive Reasoning — The ability to apply general rules to specific problems to produce answers that make sense.

Inductive Reasoning — The ability to combine pieces of information to form general rules or conclusions (includes finding a relationship among seemingly unrelated events).

Oral Comprehension — The ability to listen to and understand information and ideas presented through spoken words and sentences.

Written Comprehension — The ability to read and understand information and ideas presented in writing.

Mathematical Reasoning — The ability to choose the right mathematical methods or formulas to solve a problem.

Near Vision — The ability to see details at close range (within a few feet of the observer).

Problem Sensitivity — The ability to tell when something is wrong or is likely to go wrong. It does not involve solving the problem, only recognizing there is a problem.

Information Ordering — The ability to arrange things or actions in a certain order or pattern according to a specific rule or set of rules (e.g., patterns of numbers, letters, words, pictures, mathematical operations).

Oral Expression — The ability to communicate information and ideas in speaking so others will understand.

Written Expression — The ability to communicate information and ideas in writing so others will understand.

back to top

Work Activities

Documenting/Recording Information — Entering, transcribing, recording, storing, or maintaining information in written or electronic/magnetic form.

Interacting With Computers — Using computers and computer systems (including hardware and software) to program, write software, set up functions, enter data, or process information.

Communicating with Supervisors, Peers, or Subordinates — Providing information to supervisors, co-workers, and subordinates by telephone, in written form, e-mail, or in person.

Analyzing Data or Information — Identifying the underlying principles, reasons, or facts of information by breaking down information or data into separate parts.

Processing Information — Compiling, coding, categorizing, calculating, tabulating, auditing, or verifying information or data.

Identifying Objects, Actions, and Events — Identifying information by categorizing, estimating, recognizing differences or similarities, and detecting changes in circumstances or events.

Evaluating Information to Determine Compliance with Standards — Using relevant information and individual judgment to determine whether events or processes comply with laws, regulations, or standards.

Monitor Processes, Materials, or Surroundings — Monitoring and reviewing information from materials, events, or the environment, to detect or assess problems.

Getting Information — Observing, receiving, and otherwise obtaining information from all relevant sources.

Making Decisions and Solving Problems — Analyzing information and evaluating results to choose the best solution and solve problems.

back to top

Work Context

Electronic Mail — 90% responded "Every day."

Indoors, Environmentally Controlled — 93% responded "Every day."

Wear Common Protective or Safety Equipment such as Safety Shoes, Glasses, Gloves, Hearing Protection, Hard Hats, or Life Jackets — 82% responded "Every day."

Face-to-Face Discussions — 73% responded "Every day."

Importance of Being Exact or Accurate — 68% responded "Extremely important."

Exposed to Hazardous Conditions — 79% responded "Every day."

Contact With Others — 48% responded "Constant contact with others."

Telephone — 43% responded "Every day."

Exposed to Contaminants — 52% responded "Every day."

Structured versus Unstructured Work — 41% responded "A lot of freedom."

back to top

Job Zone

Title	Job Zone Four: Considerable Preparation Needed
Education	Most of these occupations require a four-year bachelor's degree, but some do not.
Related Experience	A considerable amount of work-related skill, knowledge, or experience is needed for these occupations. For example, an accountant must complete four years of college and work for several years in accounting to be considered qualified.
Job Training	Employees in these occupations usually need several years of work-related experience, on-the-job training, and/or vocational training.
Job Zone Examples	Many of these occupations involve coordinating, supervising, managing, or training others. Examples include accountants, sales managers, database administrators, teachers, chemists, art directors, and cost estimators.
SVP Range	(7.0 to < 8.0)

back to top

Education

Percentage of Respondents	Education Level Required
86	Bachelor's degree
7	Master's degree
4	Associate's degree

This occupation may require a background in the following science, technology, engineering, and mathematics (STEM) educational disciplines:

Chemistry — Analytical Chemistry; Chemical Physics; Chemistry; Inorganic Chemistry; Organic Chemistry; Physical and Theoretical Chemistry (see all 7 programs)

Physics/Astronomy — Chemical Physics

back to top

Credentials

Find Training | Find Certifications | Find Licenses

back to top

Interests

Interest code: **IRC**

Investigative — Investigative occupations frequently involve working with ideas, and require an extensive amount of thinking. These occupations can involve searching for facts and figuring out problems mentally.

Realistic — Realistic occupations frequently involve work activities that include practical, hands-on problems and solutions. They often deal with plants, animals, and real-world materials like wood, tools, and machinery. Many of the occupations require working outside, and do not involve a lot of paperwork or working closely with others.

Conventional — Conventional occupations frequently involve following set procedures and routines. These occupations can include working with data and details more than with ideas. Usually there is a clear line of authority to follow.

back to top

Work Styles

Attention to Detail — Job requires being careful about detail and thorough in completing work tasks.

Analytical Thinking — Job requires analyzing information and using logic to address work-related issues and problems.

Integrity — Job requires being honest and ethical.

Dependability — Job requires being reliable, responsible, and dependable, and fulfilling obligations.

Adaptability/Flexibility — Job requires being open to change (positive or negative) and to considerable variety in the workplace.

Cooperation — Job requires being pleasant with others on the job and displaying a good-natured, cooperative attitude.

Stress Tolerance — Job requires accepting criticism and dealing calmly and effectively with high stress situations.

Initiative — Job requires a willingness to take on responsibilities and challenges.

Achievement/Effort — Job requires establishing and maintaining personally challenging achievement goals and exerting effort toward mastering tasks.

Independence — Job requires developing one's own ways of doing things, guiding oneself with little or no supervision, and depending on oneself to get things done.

back to top

Work Values

Achievement — Occupations that satisfy this work value are results oriented and allow employees to use their strongest abilities, giving them a feeling of accomplishment. Corresponding needs are Ability Utilization and Achievement.

Independence — Occupations that satisfy this work value allow employees to work on their own and make decisions. Corresponding needs are Creativity, Responsibility and Autonomy.

Working Conditions — Occupations that sati[illegible] curity and good working conditions. Corresponding needs are Activity, Compensati[illegible] 'ariety and Working Conditions.

back to top

Related Occupations

17-2131.00	Materials Engineers
17-2199.01	Biochemical Engineers
17-2199.02	Validation Engineers Bright Outlook Green
19-2032.00	Materials Scientists
19-4021.00	Biological Technicians
19-4031.00	Chemical Technicians
19-4041.02	Geological Sample Test Technicians
19-4091.00	Environmental Science and Protection Technicians, Including Health
19-4092.00	Forensic Science Technicians
29-2011.00	Medical and Clinical Laboratory Technologists

back to top

Wages & Employment Trends

Median wages (2014)	$35.33 hourly, $73,480 annual
State wages	Local Salary Info
Employment (2012)	88,000 employees
Projected growth (2012-2022)	Slower than average (3% to 7%)
Projected job openings (2012-2022)	27,800
State trends	Employment Trends
Top industries (2012)	Manufacturing Professional, Scientific, and Technical Services

Source: Bureau of Labor Statistics 2014 wage data and 2012-2022 employment projections. "Projected growth" represents the estimated change in total employment over the projections period (2012-2022). "Projected job openings" represent openings due to growth and replacement.

back to top

Job Openings on the Web

Find Jobs | Job Banks

back to top

Sources of Additional Information

Disclaimer: Sources are listed to provide additional information on related jobs, specialties, and/or industries. Links to non-DOL Internet sites are provided for your convenience and do not constitute an endorsement.

- Chemists and Materials Scientists. Bur Department of Labor. *Occupational Outlook Handbook, 2014-15 Edition.*

- American Chemical Society (ACS), Education Division, Career Publications, 1155 16th St. NW, Washington, DC 20036. Phone: (800) 227-5558. Fax: (202) 872-4615.
- Materials Research Society (MRS), 506 Keystone Dr., Warrendale, PA 15086-7573. Phone: (724) 779-3003. Fax: (724) 779-8313.

back to top

Exhibit 11: Sample Job Advertisements

HART Employment Services
Login as: Employee | Supervisor

- Home
- About
- Goverment Certifications
- Careers
- Contact

Careers

Home → Careers

Apply Now   Send this job to a friend   Search

Long term assignment.
Pay Rate: $21.00 per hour with 2 shift differential. Total: $23.00/hr.
Working hours: Monday through Friday, 1 pm - 10pm
Education Requirement: B.S. in Chemistry or equivalent
Job duties: Chemical Analysis, Trace and Ultra-Trace Analysis, ICP-MS Elemental analysis, Sample Preparation

Balazs NanoAnalysis (http://www.balazs.com/), a division of Air Liquide Group (http://www.airliquide.com/), seeks a B.S. analytical chemist specializing in trace and ultratrace elemental analysis using ICP-MS. The candidates would preferably have prior experience with surface analysis ICP-MS, and wish to pursue a career in analytical chemistry with focus within the semiconductor industry. These are temp positions, based in Fremont, California.

Although the responsibilities of the position vary depending on the candidates' education and experiences, they generally include:

A) Perform chemical analysis for trace elements by ICP-MS;

B) Participate in development of new analytical methods

C) Responsible for the documentation of quality control standards and analytical results

D) Maintain, troubleshoot, and repair analytical instruments.

E) Meets or exceeds all company safety procedures and standards

General Requirements:

• Candidates must be legally authorized to work in the U.S.
• B.S. degree in Chemistry or equivalent education
• Minimum 2 years of laboratory experience in the industry
• Preferred 2+ years of ICP-MS trace element analysis experience
• Must be safety conscious
• Good organization skills
• Must be able to work in a team environment with good communication skills
• Ability to operate and maintain assigned laboratory equipment
• Ability to work under time pressure
• Must have initiative and be self-motivated
• Ability to change plans on short notice and work with a flexible schedule

Don't see the right job? Complete our General Application to be considered for future positions.

Chemist

Location: **US-NV-Henderson**
Job Code: **4341**
Department: **Quality**
Employment Duration: **Full time**
# of openings: **1**

Description

Olin Chlor Alkali Products has an opening at the Henderson (Las Vegas area), Nevada facility for a Chemist. This role independently evaluates, selects and applies standard engineering/scientific techniques, processes and criteria using judgment in making adaptations and modifications. As an individual contributor, the Chemist carries out complex or new assignments requiring the development of new or improved techniques and procedures and ensures overall quality control of processes, raw materials and products in line with regulatory and industry standards.

Olin Chlor Alkali is a major North American manufacturer and marketer of basic chemicals. Our 1,500 employees are encouraged to participate as if they are owners of the company and have helped shape us into one of the world's leading manufacturers of chlorine, caustic soda and related chemicals. These chemicals are core ingredients in the manufacturing of an exhaustive array of products - from pharmaceuticals to water purification to plastics, household cleaning products and even clothing - virtually any product you can imagine. But what really makes Olin special is our culture - a culture where every person is an integral part of the success of the company, where co-workers support and encourage each other, and where "valuing people" is not a slogan or a poster on the wall – it's the way we do business every day.

Essential Functions/Basic Duties:

- Provides chemistry and analytical support for quality assurance labs
- Provides technical support to division management regarding product quality issues that can impact customer requirements or specifications of products
- Develops standard operating procedures, modifies laboratory procedures and develops new analytical methods/techniques to ensure product quality
- Ensures development of quality analytical procedures, methods and standards certifying technological processes and procedures, qualifying products and supervising testing
- Develops quality policies, procedures, methodologies or modifications to ensure high quality products, processes and services
- Utilizes statistical tools to evaluate performance of methods and analytical equipment
- Coordinates with manufacturing and other internal departments to define and resolve product quality problems
- Maintains analytical equipment
- Coordinates service for laboratory equipment and instruments
- Assures adequate documentation and reporting of procedures, results and findings
- Plans, leads or coordinates quality related projects
- Independently makes decisions on problems and methodology issues and secures necessary resources
- Acts as an advisor to others as an expert in the field
- May be required to back-up Quality Supervisor/Manager
- Performs method validation
- Assists with training fellow employees as needed

Essential Job Requirements:

- Bachelor's Degree* in Chemistry, Engineering or Science-related discipline
- Master's Degree preferred
- Minimum 5 years' laboratory or quality assurance related experience
- Prior manufacturing, process or chemical plant experience highly preferred
- Good written and verbal communication skills; creative problem solving skills
- Ability to interface with all levels of employees
- Attention-to-detail, ability to interpret data, including use of statistical tools and make or recommend adjustments based on findings
- Knowledge of basic laboratory instrumentation
- Experience using highly-automated analytical instrumer and AutoTitrators
- Basic computer skills including Microsoft Office; SAP pre
- Quality data management systems or laboratory inform
- MiniTab or similar statistical softwar

- Ability to troubleshoot and perform minor maintenance on laboratory equipment preferred
- Knowledge and experience with quality programs (i.e. certification/documentation requirements, etc.) preferred

*Degree must be from a school that is accredited by an accrediting agency recognized by the Secretary of Education of the U.S. Department of Education.

Olin is an Equal Opportunity Employer. M/W/Vet/Disabled.

Apply for this Position

Send to a Friend

Are you a returning applicant?

Previous Applicants:

Email:

Password:

Add to My Jobs

If you do not remember your password click here

Back to Search Results

New Search

powered by Taleo

Our Culture | Media/Press | Other Sites | Library | Contact Us | Investor Relations | Legal Notice

In case of an emergency, in the US, contact CHEMTREC at 1-800-424-9300 or in Canada, contact Newalta at 1-800-567-7455.

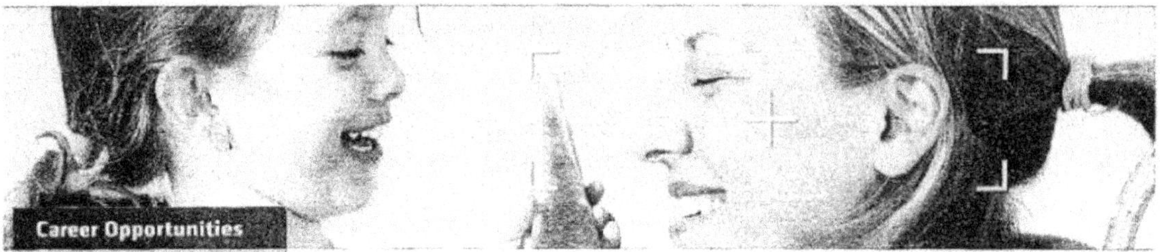

Scientist Chemist

Job ID	4334	Location	US-CA-Petaluma
Category	R&D - Dow	Pos. Type	Full Time

More information about this job:

Overview:

Valeant Pharmaceuticals International, Inc. is a diverse and decentralized pharmaceutical company that is committed to focusing on our key stakeholders while delivering consistently high performance. Our values provide the overall direction for our company, and provide us with the tools necessary to rise to any challenge by leveraging our collective hard work and effort along with our unwavering competitive spirit. These values help us set goals based on our organization's potential and what we hope it will become.

Provide general support for Formulation and Process Development / CMC Technical Operations Department. Leads in the set-up and preparation of laboratory and cGMP production work. Assist in the development of lead formulations, setting up R&D stability studies and evaluating physical properties of formulations. Document laboratory work in compliance with company policies, government regulations and prepare draft documents and technical reports. Assist in experimental design and laboratory troubleshooting. Assist technicians in meeting their tasks when necessary.

Responsibilities:

Primary Responsibilities/Functions:

- Leads specific routine or semi-routine laboratory and manufacturing operations
- Performs non-routine laboratory and manufacturing operations with minimal supervisionSets up and performs maintenance of formulation apparatus and manufacturing equipment
    - Trains technicians
-
- Identifies problems during compounding and manufacturing and recommends solutions
- Cleans laboratory and cGMP equipment, and facilities
- Assists in designing formulation development studies and manufacturing operations
- Assists in oral and written communications with both external and/or internal customers
- Requests batch materials, records receipts of the same and tracks inventory
- Prepares Purchase Order Requisitions for approval and orders supplies
- Inventories supplies and ensures restocking
- Disposes of waste in accordance with regulations and safety procedures
- Provides evaluation and analysis of laboratory data.
- Identifies problems and provides preliminary troubleshooting for formulation problems.
- Assists in study design and development of experimental protocols including R&D stability protocols
- Prepares reports for laboratory test results
- Effectively communicates with supervisors on project status and problems encountered
- Performs accurate calculations and documents work in compliance with DPSI procedures
- Performs peer review of data for other staff members
- May provide training, supervision and scheduling assistance for Technicians

Career Progress

Progression in the [illegible] nt / CMC Technical Operations to Research Scientist is [illegible] nical training, education and organizational [illegible] needs. The Research Scientist is well versed in formulation development, has developed troubleshooting skills and Technical project leadership abilities. The Research Scientist assumes a greater responsibility for the scientific integrity and regulatory compliance of the work performed and supervises technicians routinely. The degree of job complexity typically progresses with each level. For progression to Research Scientist an individual must show capacity to independently perform:

- design of experiments, conduct, and interpretation of data
- develop experimental protocols including R&D protocols
- written approvable reports for laboratory test results
- communications with supervisors on project status and problems encountered
- accurate calculations and to document work in compliance with DPSI procedures and train others
- peer review of data for other staff members
- to fulfill the expectations typical of Research Scientist (as described in Research Scientist job description)

Qualifications:

Job Requirements:

- Ability to work in accordance with written procedures
    - Assists in developing written procedures for new tasks
    - Ability to clearly document the work performed
        - Ability to effectively communicate with Supervisor, and internal and external team members
        - Ability to train and supervise technicians in conducting routine and semi-routine tasks
        - Organized and able to perform duties in a timely manner
        - Safety minded in performance of duties
            - Quality minded with ability to perform work with accuracy and in accordance with established procedures
            - Willingness to learn, follow directions and take on challenging tasks with minimal supervision
            - Reliable, trustworthy and a role model for technicians
            - Capable of assisting in planning and executing laboratory experiments and manufacturing operations
            - Ability to work on problems of diverse scope where analysis of situations or data requim evaluation of identifiable factors
            - Ability to work with no instructions on routine work and general instructions on new assignments

Essential Functions:

- Must have sufficient manual dexterity to perform laboratory testing in a manner to provide precise and accurate results and work in a safe manner
- Vision must be suitable for performing detailed inspections
- May be required to move items weighing up to 25 lbs.
- May be required to stand for long periods of time to perform laboratory work
- Individual is required to wear and use appropriate protective equipment in laboratory areas
- Must be able to work with standard laboratory chemicals under normal safety precautions and work with hazardous chemicals after proper training
- Must be able to work with computers and general laboratory instrumentation
- Able to communicate clearly and effectively both verbally and in writing

Required Education/Experience/Training:

- Bachelor's in Pharmacy, Chemistry or equivalent with 0-3 years of relevant experience in formulation development.
- Associate degree (AA) or equivalent with emphasis on technical and computer related courses and at >7 years of experience
- HS diploma or GED with >10 years of industrial experience and at least 5 years at DPSI

Valeant is an EEO/AA employer M/F/D/V

SECTION 4:
Labor Condition Application

Brian D. Lerner <blerner@californiaimmigration.us>

LCA: Case Number: I-200-15089-590641 Received: 2015-03-31 17:57:50.0

tlc.chicago@dol.gov <tlc.chicago@dol.gov> Tue, Mar 31, 2015 at 2:57 PM
To:
Cc: BLERNER@californiaimmigration.us

To:
INLAND EMPIRE LIVER FOUNDATION
2006 N RIVERSIDE AVE
SUITE A
RIALTO, CA 92377
UNITED STATES OF AMERICA Re: Case Number: I-200-15089-590641 Received: 2015-03-31 17:57:50.0This is a confirmation email that the ETA Form 9035E - Labor Condition Application for Nonimmigrant Workers covering 1 worker(s) for the position of RESEARCH CHEMIST during the period of employment beginning 09/29/2015 through 09/29/2018 (case number I-200-15089-590641) has been received and submitted for processing by the U.S. Department of Labor (Department).Important Notice: In accordance with Federal regulations at 20 C.F.R. 655.740(a), where all required items on the ETA Form 9035E have been completed and the form does not contain obvious inaccuracies, the Department is required to make a determination to certify or not certify the form within 7 working days of the date it is received by the Department [INA 212(t)(2)(C); 8 U.S.C. 1182(t)(2)(C)]. If you have not received a final determination by email within 7 working days, you may check the status of your Labor Condition Application by logging onto the iCERT System at http://iCERT.doleta.gov. You may also check the status of your application at any time after submission by accessing your account on the iCERT System. If you cannot obtain status of your LCA from the iCERT System, please contact the LCA Help Desk at LCA.Chicago@dol.gov.

SECTION 5:
Supporting Employer Applicant Declaration

INLAND EMPIRE LIVER FOUNDATION

March 30, 2015

USCIS
California Service Center
Attention: I-129/H-1B CAP
24000 Avila Road
2nd Floor, Rm. 2312
Laguna Niguel, CA 92677

Re: Petition for a Non-Immigrant Worker, H-1B Classification
Petitioner: Inland Empire Liver Foundation
Beneficiary: Mr. Abdulmunem [redacted]
Position: Chemist

Dear USCIS Officer in Charge:

Inland Empire Liver Foundation wishes to petition U.S. Citizenship and Immigration Services for H-1B nonimmigrant classification on behalf of Mr. who will be temporarily employed as a Research Chemist at our outpatient clinic facilities in Rialto, California.

U.S. EMPLOYER

Inland Empire Liver Foundation (hereinafter, "The Foundation") is an outpatient clinic specializing in the education, assistance, and support of individuals diagnosed with liver disease. We provide the latest news from a variety of trusted sources, answers to FAQ's about liver disease, local physician referrals, access to clinical trials, live chat, and more. We help match patients with clinical trials and serve as a center where individuals may come and participate in forums and support groups. We pride ourselves on being on the forefront of treatments and diagnostic testing. Our in-house pharmacy is available for prescription pick-ups for the comfort and ease of our clientele.

H-1B SPECIALITY OCCUPATION

Due to the growing popularity for out-patient clinics over traditional hospital visits, there has been notable increase in our incoming patients, it is urgent that The Foundation hires a part-time Research Chemist to keep up with the demands of this influx upon our laboratory. The Foundation wishes to employ Mr. [redacted] to fit this vacant position.

As a Research Chemist, Mr. [redacted] will be responsible for scientific research and development services including conducting tests and making determinations to aid our medical professionals in executing the top-of-the-line patient care The Foundation is known for. Further, he will be responsible for the part-time management of our laboratory, in preparing reports as well as overseeing a team of three research coordinators and one medical assistant.

Specifically, he will:

- Maintain laboratory instruments to ensure proper working order and troubleshoot malfunctions when needed.
- Prepare solutions for laboratory personnel to conduct tests.
- Evaluate laboratory safety procedures to ensure compliance with standards or to make improvements as needed.
- Compile and analyze test information to determine process efficiency and to diagnose malfunctions.
- Write technical papers and reports and specifications for processes and tests.
- Confer with scientists and medical professionals to conduct analyses of research projects, interpret test results, or develop nonstandard tests.
- Develop, improve, and customize analytical research methods.
- Attend liver transplant and hepatitis C patient support groups.
- Track clinical trials medications and enter data into the electronic data capturing systems
- Report to all adverse events and serious adverse events to FDA
- Participate in all organization health care and management meetings.
- Provide annual report about drug utilization and quality improvement
- Manage a team of three research coordinators and one medical assistant.

iELF
INLAND EMPIRE
LIVER FOUNDATION

Below please find evidence of The Foundation's specialty occupation as required under 8 CFR 214.3(h)(iii)(A).

Federal regulations define a specialty occupation as one that requires "theoretical and practical application of a body of highly specialized knowledge" which requires the "attainment of a bachelor's degree or higher in the specialty as a minimum for entry into the occupation." A specialty occupation may be found if the petitioner satisfies one of the four criteria outlined in 8 CFR 214.2(h)(4)(iii)(A) as follows: (1) a baccalaureate or higher degree or its equivalent is normally the minimum requirement for entry into the particular position; (2) the degree requirement is common to the industry in parallel positions among similar organizations or, in the alternative, an employer may show that its particular position is so complex or unique that it can be performed only by an individual with a degree; (3) the employer normally requires a degree or its equivalent for the position; or (4) the nature of the specific duties is so specialized and complex that knowledge required to perform the duties is usually associated with the attainment of a baccalaureate or higher degree.

A baccalaureate or higher degree or its equivalent is normally the minimum requirement for entry into the particular position;

Most candidates for a Chemist positions must possess at least a baccalaureate degree or its equivalent in the Chemistry sciences. Historically, the CSC has looked to the U.S. Department of Labor's ("DOL") Occupational Outlook Handbook ("OOH") and O*NET Online Occupational Database ("O*NET") in determining whether a position requires a bachelor's degree. The O*NET indicates the position of Chemist falls under the DOL category of "Chemist" (OES/SOC 19-2031), which has been classified under "Job Zone 4" and accorded and SVP range of "7 to 8", which corresponds to 4 years of standard vocational preparation. The DOL has consistently considered positions classified under Job Zone 4 and with an SVP rating of "7" as minimally requiring a baccalaureate degree. The O*NET indicates "Most of these occupations require a four-year bachelor's degree" and that "A considerable amount of work-related skill, knowledge, or experience is needed for these occupations. For example, an accountant must complete four years of college and work for several years in accounting to be considered qualified." Of the respondents who participated in O*NET's survey of this occupation, 86% indicated these positions require a bachelor's degree and 7% indicated the position required a master's degree. The OOH's interpretation of the position is consistent with the O*NET in stating "a bachelor's degree in chemistry or in a related field is needed for entry-level chemist jobs". This is a necessity because Chemists need strong complex problem solving, critical thinking, quality control analysis, and deductive reasoning. These skills will be critical in performing research, conducting tests, and in collecting and analyzing data, all of which require the use of techniques in chemistry and mathematics. These skills are typically obtained while earning a four-year

iELF
INLAND EMPIRE
LIVER FOUNDATION

bachelor's degree in Chemistry or a closely related discipline. As such, a bachelor's degree or its equivalent is minimally necessary for entry into this position.

The degree requirement is common to the industry in parallel positions among similar organizations

The requirement of a bachelor's degree for a Chemist is common to almost all scientific research and development services positions in laboratories, hospitals, private practices and out patient clinics, and in parallel positions and among similar organizations.

Chemists may be referred to with different titles and according to O*NET, reported job titles for the position include Air Quality Chemist, Analytical Chemist, Chemical Laboratory Scientist, Chemist, Forensic Chemist, Forensic Scientist, Quality Control Chemist (QC Chemist), Research Chemist, Scientist, and Senior Chemist.

We have therefore attached job announcements by companies with full laboratory facilities in the fields of pharmaceuticals and chemical research for Research Chemist positions or for positions which duties and responsibilities are the same or similar to those of a Research Chemist.

Balazs NanoAnalysis offers the most complete line of analytical services and clean manufacturing solutions for advancing high technology products. The company has a job opening for the position of a Chemist and summarizes its duties as "Perform chemical analysis for trace elements by ICP-MS, participate in development of new analytical methods, responsible for the documentation of quality control standards and analytical results, and meets or exceeds all company safety procedures and standards" amongst others.

For this position a B.S. degree in Chemistry or equivalent education is required.

Olin Chlor Alkali is a major North American manufacturer and marketer of basic chemicals. The company has a job opening for the position of a Chemist and summarizes its duties as "provides chemistry and analytical support for quality assurance labs, provides technical support to division management regarding product quality issues that can impact customer requirements or specifications of products, develops standard operating procedures, modifies laboratory procedures and develops new analytical methods/techniques to ensure product quality, ensures development of quality analytical procedures, methods and standards certifying technological processes and procedures, qualifying products and supervising testing, and develops quality policies, procedures, methodologies or modifications to ensure high quality products, processes and services."

For this position a Bachelor's Degree in Chemistry, Engineering or Science-related discipline is required.

Valeant Pharmaceuticals International, Inc. is a diverse and decentralized pharmaceutical company that is committed to focusing on our key stakeholders while delivering consistently high performance. The company has posted a job opening for the position of Scientist Chemist and summarizes its duties as "...Disposes of waste in accordance with regulations and safety procedure, Provides evaluation and analysis of laboratory data, Identifies problems and provides preliminary troubleshooting for formulation problems, identifies problems during compounding and manufacturing and recommends solutions, and may provide training, supervision and scheduling assistance for Technicians" amongst others.

For this position, the company requires a Bachelor's Degree in Pharmacy, Chemistry or its equivalent.

As one can readily see in the attached ads, the job descriptions listed are consistent with the job description of the Research Chemist position The Foundation wishes to fill. Each employer requires a bachelor's degree for entry into the available position. It is, therefore, reasonable to conclude that the degree requirement is common in the industry among similar organizations for parallel positions.

The employer normally requires a degree or its equivalent for the position.

The Foundation normally requires a bachelor's degree in chemistry or its equivalent for the position of Research Chemist. The Foundation seeks to maintain its reputation as a leader in outpatient services for patients with liver disease – which includes employing only individuals who possess at least a bachelor's degree in chemistry. Given its reputation in the area, The Foundation requires a professional to do the work of a Research Chemist to ensure that our clients get the highest quality care and assistance. Hence, the Foundation has established a standard for hiring only candidates who meet this minimum educational requirement.

It is, therefore, reasonable to conclude that our degree requirement is in conformance with USCIS's specialty occupation requirements and that the company's normal policy is to hire research chemists possessing the equivalent of a baccalaureate degree for this position.

The nature of the specific duties is so specialized and complex that knowledge required to perform the duties is usually associated with the attainment of a bachelor's or similar degree.

The duties of a Research Chemist with The Foundation are so specialized and complex that the knowledge required to perform them is usually associated with the attainment of a bachelor's degree. The nature of the job duties are such that they require a level of skill typically attained from completing a bachelor's degree in Chemistry or a similar field.

To accomplish the duties and responsibilities of a Research Chemist in our facility, the candidate must use scientific rules and methods to solve problems, apply logic and reasoning to identify the strengths and weaknesses of alternative solutions, conclusions or approaches to problems, complex problem solving skills, ability to take in and assess new information swiftly and accurately, and strong managerial expertise. These skills and knowledge are learned and refined through courses in chemistry, other sciences and mathematics. The level of skills in research and science require college-level academic training, including knowledge that is acquired in classes offered at Bachelor's Chemistry and like sciences programs.

The Research Chemist's duties and responsibilities for The Foundation require strong analytical and writing skills. He must be able to translate information he has gathered into a report that would be meaningful for medical professionals in advancing diagnostic tactics and furthering the treatment of liver disease. He must be detail-oriented and must possess logical reasoning and a critical mind.

It is clear that these responsibilities/skills require a level of technical expertise and sophistication that is not possessed by someone lacking a bachelor's degree. Only someone with a breadth of knowledge generally obtained while completing a bachelor's degree program or its equivalent in Chemistry or like sciences, or in a related discipline is qualified to perform these job duties at our organization. These duties are beyond the ability of a candidate not possessing the educational requirements requested.

BENEFICIARY'S QUALIFICATIONS

Mr. Abdulmunem is uniquely qualified for entry into the Research Chemist position we wish to fill, based on his education. The rare combination of his knowledge and skills in the field of Research Chemistry and Management are invaluable for this position.

After enrolling and completing four years of academic coursework and examinations at the University of Aleppo, Syria, he obtained his diploma in 1998, demonstrating that he completed his Bachelor of Pharmaceutical Chemistry. While at University, he took up and successfully completed subjects in Chemistry, Mathematics, Pharmaceutical Studies. According to an attached evaluation performed by Educational Credentials Evaluators, Inc. Mr.

university studies is equivalent to a U.S. Bachelor's degree in Pharmacy Chemistry.

In 2001, Mr. became a licensed pharmacist in Syria and became the owner and manager of a pharmacy from 2001-2013. He then went on to enroll in the University of California, Los Angeles's UCLA Extension's General Business and Management program.

TERMS OF EMPLOYMENT

A Labor Condition Application ("LCA") has been filed with the U.S. Department of Labor's Employment Training Administration and the original Form ETA-9035 is enclosed with this petition. An approval of this application is expected imminently. The Foundation will comply with all labor condition statements contained in said attestation and will make available for examination a copy of the LCA, all required supporting documents, and this H-1B petition.

Mr. will be employed in the position of part-time Research Chemist for a period of three years, during which time he will be paid an annual salary equivalent to that as set forth in the certified labor condition application plus standard company benefits.

The Foundation's worksite is located in Rialto, California at the address listed on Form I-129. Mr. will perform the stated job duties at the work site address alone and not at any third-party or clients sites. As part of his regular job duties, Mr. will attend off-site scientific and research conferences and represent The Foundation in his capacity as a Research Chemist at off-site meetings as necessary. These duties are part of the employee's job functions and any related travel will be casual, short-term, and occasional in nature.

Mr. will be directly employed by The Foundation and there will be no intermediary employment agencies between them. As the direct employer of Mr. The Foundation will be solely responsible for his hiring, pay, and termination and will control his work in accordance with an employer-employee relationship. Mr. will report to The Foundation's chief Medical Director and no other intermediary supervisor at The Foundation or outside of The Foundation. The employment relationship will be terminable at will by either Mr. or The Foundation. The Foundation retains the sole authority to fire Mr. and to set rules and regulations on his work. If job performance issues arise, The Foundation has the exclusive authority to take corrective action including, but not limited to, terminating Mr. employment. Mr. has no role in hiring or paying workers. Mr. sole responsibility is to perform the job duties listed herein.

iELF
INLAND EMPIRE LIVER FOUNDATION

The Foundation's financial health is solid and, according to financial projections, the company can generate work for Mr. [redacted] through the entirety of the H-1B validity period and pay the prevailing wage as established by the U.S. Department of Labor. As with any company, if The Foundation cannot generate enough work to employ Mr. [redacted] consistent with its attestations in its H-1B petition, it will terminate his employment and withdraw the H-1B petition.

Our organization finds Mr. [redacted] qualified for the position we wish to fill.

The Foundation wishes to employ Mr. [redacted] as a part-time Research Chemist who will work fifteen (15) hours a week for a period of three years. He will receive an annual wage as set forth in the certified labor conditions application with standard benefits. The Foundation will pay Mr. [redacted] return transportation costs in accordance with federal immigration laws.

Thank you for your consideration of this matter.

Very truly yours,

Zeid Kayali
Medical Director
Inland Empire Liver Foundation

www.ingramcontent.com/pod-product-compliance
Lightning Source LLC
Chambersburg PA
CBHW061356240926
51846CB00007B/1427
* 9 7 8 1 9 4 8 7 7 4 8 6 4 *